# Anxiety and Depression:
## 42 Essays on Overcoming the Wild Moods

Marty L. Cooper, MFT

Visit my website at:
**www.mlcooper.com**

Feel free to contact me at:
**martycooper@mlcooper.com**

## DEDICATION

To my wife, Heather, my life's prime blessing.
And to my friends and teachers, who have taught me, through
pain and pleasure, what it means, and what it costs,
to live a life free from the Wild Moods.

# TABLE OF CONTENTS

## INTRODUCTION

## SECTION 1: INSPIRATION

## SECTION 2: CONTEXT

[There is] this myth that I can rest in some assuredness, that I will never again feel insecure, or feel fear, or feel doubt, or feel those emotions we don't want to feel—if I'm truly enlightened, I will never feel those emotions. Forget it. That's not it. That's the pipe dream, that's the opium that's sold to the masses. And they eat it up and they never get there and they end up disillusioned. That's not how it works.

Freedom is never freedom from. If freedom is freedom *from* anything, it's not freedom at all. It's freedom *to*.

Are you free enough to be afraid? Are you free enough to feel insecure? Are you free enough not to know? You see what I mean? Are you free enough to know that you can't know? Are you free enough to be totally comfortable knowing that you can't know what's around the next corner, how you will feel about it, how you will respond to it, that you literally can't know. Are you free enough to be totally at ease and comfortable with the way things actually are? That's freedom. The other thing is the ego's *idea* of freedom.

--*Adyashanti*

# INTRODUCTION:
# THE WHAT, WHY, AND HOW OF THIS BOOK

Greetings! I'm so happy that you've picked up this book because it means you're looking for a way to tame the (as I refer to them) Wild Moods of anxiety and depression. Good for you, because what you're acting on by opening this book is both the desire and a real intuition that there is a way out of the swirls and eddies of these painful states. As one who has struggled with the Wild Moods, I can vouch for the reality that these moods can be disarmed and that life can be put not on just on a survival footing, but can be built on a basis of happiness and satisfaction.

But as you'll see in the essays below, one of the central contentions of this book is that *making this change takes work and intention and support.* It takes learning how you participate in feeding these Wild Moods, and acceptance of both the mere existence of these moods (which can be a huge chunk of the work) as well as how your habits of life contribute to the wildness of the Wild Moods. Now, all that can be a bit to swallow if you haven't encountered the idea before, because what I'm basically saying is that if you've had *ongoing* depression and anxiety, there's a deep way in which, in order to tame these Wild Moods, your *you* has to change.

Now, since the Wild Moods are so laced through with "negative" emotions— shame, guilt, blame, recrimination, regrets, etc., all the heavy ones—then the assertion that *you* have to change can come with, as my grandmother used to put it, a mighty big wallop. But my intention is not to inflict a wallop. Rather, in my mind, coming from my fundamental rootedness in mindfulness meditation practice, there really is no shame or blame to be had, only an opportunity to notice where we participate in our own suffering, and learn different ways to change our suffering.

Really, that all. The essays below are pragmatic to the core: what's happening, what's getting in the way, and how to change it. Period.

**What's here and how to approach the book**

"Taming the Wild Moods" is a compilation drawn from a blog I wrote for about a year, around 2007-2008. The material which has been culled, organized, edited (and re-edited) to make it more cogent and reflective of my current approach and thinking. The essay form is reflective of that; each essay was a blog entry, and thus though thematically they are all of a piece, because I wrote weekly, the focus points vary quite a bit.

So what you'll find below are 42 essays organized into three main sections: Inspiration, Context, and Exercises (explained below). As you'll see, each essay ranges from real practical life stuff (goal setting and envisioning) to real macro-level stuff (who we are in relation to the cosmos). And this is intentional, because one of the antidotes to the narrowness and "dumbness" of depression and anxiety is simply its opposite: breadth and complexity. So I don't shy away from talking about spirituality, and quoting spiritual teachers (as well as psychologists), because this question of our *relationship to life* is always embedded in the wildness of the Wild Moods. It's not at all important in what form the question is engaged—I'm inspired by Buddhism and so-called "non-dual" teachings, so that's what gets me moving—but more that the question of meaning *is* engaged.

**Explanation of the Sections**

*Inspiration*, as I address it in Section 1, is not intended as any kind of palliative, or as something to paper over suffering. Not at all! It's not one big happy world; suffering, as you know, is pervasive and profound. So here, the intention of focusing on inspiration is in line with the base meaning of the word, "to breathe in," and what is being breathed in is an expression of reality and truth. Not dogma—there's very little use in that, when one is trying to tame the Wild Moods—but rather a pointing to the *reality* of connectedness, meaning, and purpose as a base human truth that can, more and more, be experienced. This focus on inspiration is, actually, not an option in this approach to anxiety and depression; inspiration is not the add-on element in this therapy, something that can be taken or left. Rather, the *felt* experience of inspiration is essential to unwind the falsities of anxiety and depression, whose claim is that you, people, and life in general are worthless and hopeless.

*Context*, the focus of Section 2, is the bulk of the book, and consists of essays talking about the Wild Moods from different angles, different ways of looking at and thinking about anxiety and depression. Most essays do not lay out specific strategies or techniques per se, but are intended more to question, backlight, chip away at the crusty notions at the core of the Wild Moods in order to open space and possibility for action. These essays are about one's *orientation* or *attitude* towards anxiety and depression, and as you'll come to see, how one relates to the Wild Moods is *much* more important to changing these moods than finding the perfect tool that allows you to perfectly control or excise them.

*Exercises*, Section 3, consists of a handful of essays with specific practices or experiments to cultivate certain insights or skills in relation to the Wild Moods. This is not the main part of the book because, as I said above, attitude is more important than control. An accepting, non-aggressive approach (not passive—we can be intense in our actions) gives the base from which we experiment with ways to change and understand these moods. And this is *very* important, as I argue below.

**Suggestions on how to read the book**

As you'll see in the table of contents, each essay has a title, and then a description, because this book is not intended to be read sequentially, but rather in measured amounts according to what interests you. The descriptions are there to flesh out the focus of the essay, in order to allow you find what interests you. My suggestion is to read the first essay, "Wily Kindness," which summarizes the approach of the whole book, and then from there jump in wherever the water seems most inviting.

Also, please give yourself time to digest and work with what you read: there's a lot going on in most of these essays, and they're intended to spark, provoke, or inspire you, so let yourself engage them creatively, with curiosity and openness. And if there are exercises, I'd really encourage you to set aside some time to do them, both for their particular use, as well as to practice engagement per se. Turning towards life, in whatever its form, is in itself an act of taming the Wild Moods.

**My orientation**

So just a quick note on myself before letting you go from the atrium. I'm a licensed psychotherapist in private practice in San Francisco, CA, and have been treating people with ongoing anxiety and depression for about the last 10 years.

My background is in Buddhist psychology and practice, specifically Vipassana ("Insight") meditation practice, which has been popularized in a non-sectarian form by Jon Kabat-Zinn and his colleagues at the University of Massachusetts. I have been teaching meditation classes from the Mindfulness-Based Cognitive Therapy for Depression (MBCT) perspective for a number of years now (derived from Kabat-Zinn's work). This approach contextualizes a lot of what you'll read below.

Personally, I struggled with the Wild Moods for many years, back into my childhood, and can honestly say that these moods are not only tamed, but substantially domesticated. Here and there these moods get a little rambunctious and need more attention—chronic anxiety and depression does not simply evaporate—but what I've learned and practiced is consistently effective in getting a leash on these moods, and informs all the essays in this book.

And what I've learned, and what is so embedded in mindfulness practice, is that, in terms of effectiveness, *attitude trumps control.* And also what I started with: in order to uproot (not simply control) the Wild Moods, in some ways, how we think of ourselves has to change. Initially this feels like an affront, but in time one comes to experience it as a profound relief. Believe it or not.

# 1: OVERVIEW:
# INTRODUCTION TO WILY KINDNESS

My experience has been that when you are really effectively dealing with depression and anxiety, what you're doing is a kind of *wily kindness*. Much of the suffering in these states (i.e., the often linked states of depression and anxiety) comes not so much from their natures, as from how we struggle with the states themselves. It's as if you're arm wrestling a rose bush—if you enter the fight, you're going to end it bleeding.

*Wily kindness* is looking at your own experience without hostility, but also without blinders. With just the *kindness*, you often will lack the motivation or energy to actually get things done in your life. And with just the *wily,* you might be able to punch through the anxiety/depression, but underneath, the hatred and struggle with, and the lack of *acceptance of,* these states will cause you deep suffering.

I remember hearing an interview with an environmental activist who had been imprisoned in Arizona. She talked about the struggles of prison life, and about her own growth in the midst of it. The quote that has stuck with me for all these years is, "I've learned to love people whom I cannot trust." The same could be said of skillful management of anxiety/depression, because the claims made by these states are deeply untrustworthy. And yet to hate them because of the ignorance of their claims is to jump right in with the roses—there's no winning that fight.

What are these claims? They usually sound something like, "The world is empty." "You are not worthy (of happiness, of love, of companionship, of grace, of joy)." "There is danger *everywhere*, so if you want to survive, be *small!*" "You can't possibly do..." "Be exposed and you'll be eaten." "No one loves you." "There's no way to solve your suffering." "It's all hopeless and you'd better just face it." Often these claims will be phrased as "I...," but it's really anxiety and/or depression that is speaking, and we just get confused about us not being the same as these states.

So with *wily kindness*, you practice recognizing that these messages are simply false (in the beginning, this takes faith on your part, and support from others to help you believe this). But you also hold onto the fact that if you hate these messages because of this falseness, you are making more suffering for yourself.

This, admittedly, is a bit tricky, because if you've suffered with these states for a long time, particularly if the anxiety/depression began in childhood, then you've likely come to believe that the only thing keeping you from deep depression and anxiety is fighting these moods tooth and nail. But to move towards actually resolving and dissolving anxiety and depression, you have to learn to approach your moods with *kindness*, not animosity. Tall order? Only if you haven't yet experienced it. Once you really feel how different it is to sit with these states in watchful acceptance, and then act on them with the kind of attitude you'd take towards a beloved, if wayward child, then it becomes clear how your strategy of struggle comes at a cost.

As an experiment (and an experimental attitude is extremely important in mastering these states), you can try the following exercise. (Though if you start getting overwhelmed, stop the exercise and do whatever is soothing to you. When you're overwhelmed, it's not only painful, but you can't really do your work. Be gentle with yourself).

1) Get physically comfortable.

2) Feel whatever depression/anxiety current is accompanying you (as thoughts, emotions, and physical sensations).

3) Start with the phrase, "Depression/anxiety, you are not my enemy," and try to say this with as much conviction as you can find.

4) Notice if there are changes in your state (again, as thoughts, emotions, sensations).

5) Change the phrase and see if you can find something that feels truer. (For example, "Depression/anxiety, though you are difficult companions, I choose not to fight you.")

6) Keep doing this until you find a phrasing that rings as believably as you're going to find (for some, it might be "I'm willing to consider that I'm not totally the same as these experiences...which suck!"—that's fine, as long as it's the truth for you).

# SECTION 1: INSPIRATION

## ESSAY 2:  TAKING RESPONSIBILITY
## FOR ONE'S SUFFERING

While I was running in Golden Gate Park, a traditional Zen story cam to mind, which goes something like this:

### *Eating the Blame*

> Circumstances arose one day which delayed preparation of the dinner for a Zen master, Fugai, and his followers.  In haste, the cook went to the garden with his curved knife and cut off the tops of green vegetables, chopped everything together, and made soup, unaware that in his haste he had included a part of a snake with the vegetables.

> The followers of Fugai thought they had never tasted such great soup.  But when the master himself found the snake's head in his bowl, he summoned the cook.  "What is this?" he demanded, holding up the head of the snake.

> "Oh, thank you, master," replied the cook, taking the morsel and eating it quickly.

That day in the park was just gorgeous; crisp blue skies, and the deep greens of the cypress and eucalyptus trees near Stowe Lake, the air clean from a recent rain.  Yet a funk had crept into my psyche that kind of oozed out onto all those same gorgeous elements around me, so that the day was a funk-filled one.  Funk surrounded me, misted down from the canopy, boiled up from the asphalt, oozed like pitch out of the trees.

But the thought came as I padded along:  there's no funk out there; it's all inside, so eat the blame.  It made sense in the moment so I allowed the unpleasantness I felt to pull in, like rolling in a dozen garden hoses...um, but more quickly. And what revealed itself was both the gorgeousness of the day in sensual terms, but also its qualities of openness, potential, and something close to comradeship. The world seemed, unlike a few minutes before, just fine with me running it and through it, and was happily sharing what it had to share, rather than somehow depriving me of contentment.

The funk, however, did not magically disappear, but it did—and in my experience, always does—transform. Instead of me being in *it*, it was in *me*. That makes a tremendous difference. If Buddha was right in saying that suffering is rooted in ignorance of reality, and what is real is that all things (and therefore their boundaries/definitions) are essentially unified, then suffering is always going to involve some experience of isolation.

By "eating the blame" in this sense, by not casting responsibility out over the world's denizens, by recognizing that in a radical sense, there is no blame out there, we remain connected to our world, which is us. We also are not deluded about the cure for our suffering. We realize it is not a matter of cutting down the oppressive trees, or turning up the iPod, or going home and hiding under a blanket, but of seeing the way we are unconsciously constructing our own pain, most especially by projecting it out onto the world.

When I remember that it is, at the end of the day, *my* snake head, so there's also a great energetic relief. Taking responsibility for what is yours frees up the energy that otherwise goes into defending against the guilty parties that are "making" you suffer; ironically, by owning what is yours, the force fields shut down and that juice goes back into the power grid.

So: the practice is that, when you see the snake head floating in the soup of life, grab yourself a spoon and enjoy!

# ESSAY 3: MOVING WITH EASE AND SIMPLICITY

The other day, while talking with my wife and an old friend, a fragment of memory was dislodged from some underground crevice and shot up to the surface of my mind, vivid in its single detail: the image of Thich Nhat Hahn, onstage in Berkeley, adjusting his robe.

The actual event happened shortly after 9/11. My friend and colleague took me to see the Buddhist monk give a talk, whose exact subject I'm forgetting, except for fragments of his discourse on relating to such horrible events. It was a long evening, in a hall filled with perhaps a thousand people, and I seemed to have drifted in and out of listening, and probably went to sleep.

But that one brief motion of Thich Nhat Hahn shifting his saffron robe has stuck with me. It was, in all honesty, breathtaking, and still is as I remember the experience. He was preparing for the discourse, and had just finished the introductory chanting and meditation. His monks were sitting still and waiting. Thich Nhat Hahn reached down and took the edge of his monk's robe, and quickly moved it to the side, straightened up, and commenced speaking. And that was it. Yet there was an incredible *frankness* about the motion, a sense of there being no distance between the man and the motion. That the intention to arrange his robe and its execution as a bodily act did not happen in different times and places, but were one seamless event, happening in the extremely vivid present moment. But the movement was totally without adornment or affectation, or any studied self-consciousness. This wasn't a teaching he was offering; he was just straightening a piece of cloth.

This little vignette highlights what I see as one of the core sufferings that people come to psychotherapy to deal with, namely, the awareness that there is something *sticking* between our intention and our action. There's a painful sense of disconnect from ourselves, and a recognition of lag or awkwardness in acting on our desires.

For instance, someone might come in to therapy with a desire to quit their current job, but can't find the traction to act, as if they were standing in tennis shoes on an ice skating rink.  Or another might want to deal with their sense of physical sluggishness, with an insight that their lack of freedom of motion has something to do with what's going on—or not going on—in their minds. And it seems to me that the basic goal of both these people is to unify desire and action, to find *ease* in the doing of our lives.

I remember practicing judo in college, and in the midst of a sparing session I found the "sweet spot" and tossed my opponent over my shoulder with virtually no effort.  The experience was of power without force, and both openness and action in the same motion.  There was *me* doing the throwing, but not *just* me.  Feeling deeply open to my opponent and to myself, mindful of where I was in relationship to him, and the floor, and my muscles, and the space of the room, gravity...it allowed for effortless action, and a sense of liberation.  I think that if any of us looks back through our history, we'll find such moments, and see that they often provided impetus for change and opening to something deeper in ourselves.

So it seems that all practices, including psychotherapy, aim at reminding us that it is possible to move in the world without so much struggle, and these insights intend to give us ways to practice, as it were, adjusting our various robes with ease and simplicity.

# ESSAY 4: LIFE AS FRIEND:
# THE WISDOM OF HAROLD AND MAUDE

One of my most beloved movies of all times is Harold and Maude. I've seen this movie probably a dozen or more times over the last fifteen years, and each time I see something different, or feel another resonance that mirrors a change that's happened in my life since the last viewing. But the quote below, from Maude, from one of my favorite scenes in the film, has always stayed with me. It strikes me as a beautifully concise description of the development of deep empathy, of viewing life not as an enemy to be overcome, but as a friend and fellow to embrace. This applies to anything seen as an enemy, including chronic depression and anxiety.

The great successes I've seen and had in working with these states is when this fundamental shift happens. You realize that the fight for your life perhaps needed to happen in the past, but can now be let go of, and since anxiety and depression thrive on aversion and struggle, these feelings start transforming into something entirely different.

So, to set up the scene, in case you haven't seen the film: Maude and Harold are hanging out in her railroad car home, and she tells the story of using her big umbrella to fend off thugs and bosses' lackeys on various picket lines. Suddenly she becomes uncharacteristically quiet and teary as she describes describing some old losses in her life:

> [Harold] "So you don't use the umbrella any more?" he said, breaking the silence.
> She looked at him. "No," she said softly. "Not any more."
> "No more revolts?"
> "Oh, indeed!" said Maude, sparking back to her old self. "Every day.

But I don't need a defense any more. I embrace! Still fighting for the Big Issues, but now in my small, individual way."

If you haven't seen it, it does have some hippie trappings, but don't let that scare you off. It's a very beautiful and wise film.

# ESSAY 5: THE VAST HUMAN CLIMB

A very old and dear friend had a healthy, bouncing baby boy, now two weeks old. I had the great honor of being with him and his wife a few hours after the birth, when, despite the various upheavals of the child's arrival at the hospital, a deep stillness underlay all the family visitations and the coming-and-going of medical personnel.

That stillness has not quite continued; the new parents are on a growth curve of learning to interpret "waahhaaahhaa!" and how to deal with sleep in two hour chunks. Everything seems to be progressing fairly typically, with what appears to be standard amounts of happiness and pain.

Never having spent so much time around a newborn, what it has unexpectedly surfaced is a deeper appreciation—not of the particular struggles of individuals, which I already have a deep empathy for, but of the "impersonal" struggles of human beings. Looking at this little being, with his animatronic-like movements, his inability to focus, his language of a half-dozen nuanced cries, his out of control body functions—it gets me reflecting on what a climb it is for life qua life.

Think about Mars. Maybe there were some microbes at some distant past, or maybe even now, buried under a vast plain of dust and rock and ice. There are no grasses, no trees, no insects, no mice. It's like a sterilized Mojave, with texture. Here in my own neighborhood, there must be 50 different trees, and hundreds of different species of other plants and critters. Yet at one point, Earth was as barren as Mars, and all of the present incredible diversity has arisen from a browner colored rock-and-dust.

What a climb. What intense dramas have played out just to create a mammalian body that could support cognition of a rudimentary sort. That could allow the base for the emergent psychological world, and its dramas. Could produce a brain and mind so complex that it could experience something called "depression" (rocks can't do that). All this, all the inconceivably vast play of energy and form over ungraspable spans of time, has localized in the form of my friend's newborn, in his raucously "bodied" phase.

Holding him, and knowing something about human pains and struggles, it's quite moving to imagine the vast effort that has formed him, and the efforts that will be called from him to even develop the basics, of language, movement, relationship. And then the personal struggles on top of that, finding meaning, purpose, love. Falling on your face and trying to make sense and use of it.

With this nascent being, this arc of effort is particularly poignant, and is easily forgotten or missed when looking at an adult, with all the clouds of language and personality. But my ability to type on this keyboard has a few billion year history, at least. Pretty astounding when you think about it.

## ESSAY 6: DAILY LIFE AS LIVING SACRED: THE WISDOM OF *JOHN FROM CINCINNATI*

I've been quite taken by a new show on HBO, *John from Cincinnati*, which is created by David Milch (who also created *NYPD Blue* and the stunning *Deadwood*). On the surface, it's about the lives of a family of surfers and those closest in to their pretty dysfunctional inner circle, with John being the enigmatic character who seems to bring miracles with him from his arbitrarily assigned home of Cincinnati. Examples of the miracles so far: the patriarch of the family, Mitch Yost, finds himself levitating after a morning's surfing. A parrot is resurrected from the dead, apparently by Mitch's grandson, a surfing prodigy. Well, I won't give too many spoilers.

There's no denying it's an odd and perplexing take on life. But what I find so moving is that this is not just another presentation of a struggling family. You could imagine the show going in any number of conventional directions: the slapstick comedy, the grimly realistic drama (e.g., *The Wire*), the sit-com, etc.

What I see being offered is a presentation of what this early 21st century world looks like when it is seen as life lived within a temple. That is, within a sacred space, defined as a specific area that is dedicated to a spiritual purpose. Everything within such a space can be seen as related to that purpose. For instance, think of a golden cup in the curio shop in your local mall, then the same cup on the altar at the Catholic church. It's the same object, but so different in the different contexts.

*JfC* shows sort of a beat up, dented chalice, with missing jewels and someone's graffiti scrawl, but in the church of Spirit, it sparkles and shines without actually anything changing. It's the same imperfect vessel, but now reflecting and filled with the numinous that actually contains it. And in the context of this cable program, what is the container? It's the mind of its authors and whatever light they are able to channel.

In other words, it's the *belief* that life is sacred which changes everything, which makes this show a very odd testament to Spirit rather than another joke or cynical statement. In an exaggerated, physical way (the image of Mitch the surfing patriarch hovering three inches off the beach), it's showing what life feels like when you believe (and experience) as contained in Spirit/God/The Numinous/The Ineffable (whatever name you want to use).

I once heard Adyashanti, the Zen Buddhist teacher, take a question from a student, who asked (as near as I remember), "I'm having various deeper experiences now, expansive and beautiful, but I keep worrying that I'm not really worthy of them." Adyashanti's reply was, "Don't worry, you're not worthy. Nothing you can do will make you worthy. And that's why it's such a deep grace that we all can receive."

This grace is what all these (very) flawed characters are being given, as channeled through the character of John (and the mind and heart of the writer Milch), who approaches the characters with both innocence and laser clear perception, as well as deep love and acceptance. No one in this show has earned through their deeds the forgiveness and inclusion in the universe that John (basically, the spokesman of Spirit) conveys and starts to help them experience for themselves. It's through his demonstration of life lived in the sacred that they begin to shift their vision and belief. Their *experiences* with John start turning their vision of life, their sense of where they are *actually* living.

What Milch and crew are doing with *JfC* really bears on all of our lives, especially those of us who live with depression and anxiety, whose stories about life are generally pretty bleak and scary, and therefore directly shape our choices: if you believe your house is dangling off a cliff, you'll be reluctant to dance.

In other words, our story about where we live has huge ramifications on how we live in the world. Take a look at what your story is and why it's there. And then see if you can find, in your daily experience, anything that contradicts it. For instance, if you believe it's a dog-eat-dog world, look around and see where it isn't (I'm always amazed at the *density* of small kindnesses, of people allowing me into traffic, of thanking me for something, of accepting my apology for stepping on their toes, and on and on). See if you can't experience any moments where your life, or life in general, feels like it's lit by ritual candles and filtered light through stained glass.

And when you find yourself resisting this exploration (you will), then take some time to muse on what your story is giving you that you may not want to give up. Whatever you find out, try to hold it in the spirit of *John,* with clear perception and unconditional acceptance, as a bent chalice on an altar.

# ESSAY 7: DANCING YOUR DANCE
# OUT TO THE END

The morning was crisp, the sky mostly clear over Lake Merritt; runners and walkers and lake cleaners and kids with moms and dogs—the wonderful gaggle of humans were out enjoying the morning. Once inside the United Methodist Church, though, none of the lake opera could be heard outside, and only the sky and pigeons could be seen through the windows behind Adyashanti, the morning's speaker.

Perhaps 500 people showed up on that Saturday morning to listen to the Zen Buddhist teacher, who spoke for about 45 minutes before taking questions. It's always curious what one brings away from such a talk, and if I were to go again next week, to hear the exact same talk with the exact same people, I'd probably come away with a totally different understanding. What I retained was a sense that Adyashanti seems to have truly done his work—he came across as both a sweet and spiritually uncompromising man—, as well as embodying a quote from his teacher, "Dance your dance out till the end."

Take a minute to sit with that, swirl it around in your mind and see what flavors emerge. Done?

Well, to me, what emerges is an injunction to live *honestly*, to find out what one's dance is—who one is, what one *truly* likes and loves, what work calls and which repels—and to, without apology or bargaining, be that. And be that so thoroughly that eventually your own dance is exhausted and, with no energy left, you open to something new. Meaning that the path is your self, and your self fully lived will lead to the end of your "self" and the start of something new.

It's not a philosophy of sculpting yourself to an image. There's a radical trust there that the divine is us, that Spirit is "closer than our skin," and that our own unqualified, untampered-with experience is the path to the end of suffering. As Adyashanti said to someone who, upon reaching the microphone copped to being nervous, "Just be real."

What a life, eh, where we are fully aware of ourselves without apology or explanation or defense. Like a river that has been stripped of all the boulders and trees, free to flow unhindered in a path that eventually will lead to the vastness of the ocean.

## ESSAY 8:  SEEING THROUGH EYES OF INNOCENCE

One place where psychotherapy is, to my mind, gaining immensely from Buddhist practice is in its experimenting with mindfulness techniques—i.e., experiential, here-and-now awareness—in the therapy setting.  Adyashanti (in <u>Emptiness Dancing</u>) has an interesting comment on the felt difference between experience that is filtered or un-filtered, as well as the legacy of language:

> It can be difficult to understand how thorough this innocence [of direct, unfiltered experience] is.  For example, if you are sitting in your chair and you have a certain sensation arise in your body that your mind would immediately label fear, the innocence wouldn't know that.  Even a feeling the mind would call fear isn't recognized by innocence because it's not perceiving through mind.  It would look at it like, "I'll be darned, what is this?" When you become interested in something, you move toward it.  If a sound is interesting, you lean into it.  If a smell is interesting, you sniff.  Innocence just looks with curiosity and asks, "What is it?" And it draws the sensation very close.  It discovers what that sensation is through the experience rather than through the ideas.  It's very different to experience the sensation of fear through experience rather than through the idea of it, because a word like fear has been passed down through generations—there is a transmission of mind from generation to generation—as soon as the thought comes up in your head that says "fear," it's not just about this moment; it's about countless generations of fear.

> But innocence isn't looking through thought so it's bypassing history.  Innocence is newly discovered each moment.  It's not something that the egoic mind chooses...The innocence already exists and is approaching and experiencing each moment in a totally innocent way.  When you start to touch upon it, you start to feel the childlike curiosity of it;  you find that it actually moves toward experience,

toward each thing. That's why in many religions there is the advice to be childlike (which is not childish, but childlike) because that childlikeness is always so vitally interested in what is. This is the quality of freshness we feel when we are living from no separate self.

Of course we still have a brain and we still have thoughts, so things are still learned and experiences accumulated. The egoic state of consciousness always perceives through this accumulated knowledge. The only difference in living from no separate self is that we do not perceive through that accumulation, although we can reach into it when necessary. Perceiving instead through innocence actually makes us extraordinarily capable of being wise in the moment because, in that state, the deepest wisdom of the moment arises. This wisdom belongs only to the moment and is not part of our accumulated knowledge. In Zen we call it prajna, "heart wisdom," which is a wisdom that belongs to the whole. It belongs to the moment. (p. 24-26)

# SECTION 2: CONTEXT

# ESSAY 9: FINDING THE EXPERIENCES
## WE *ACTUALLY* NEED

Sandy was flailing in the whirlpool of her anxiety. She could spot what her mind was saying—"We have to do something to stop this anxiety, but we don't have the power. But we *have to do something!* But..."—but couldn't find enough ground to pull herself out of the swirl. In a familiar desperation, she saw herself reaching out for anything to hang onto, wanting to lose herself in television or food. "Miserable," she thought, "Absolutely miserable."

This "no exit" quality of anxiety is so part and parcel of what keeps this emotion in place: our danger warnings go off because of some internal or external experience, our thoughts add to the anxiety, we can't find an immediate cure, which makes us feel even more endangered, our bodies signal more danger, our minds react, and...so on. This is the stuckness, the circular quality of this particular wild mood.

One way of coping is what Sandy found herself lunging for, the strategies she had learned help "muffle" the experience of anxiety. Overeating suppresses the physical sensations, like putting one's finger on a vibrating guitar string, and creates a thin sense of empowerment ("Well, at least I can control what I'm eating!"). Disappearing into TV does a similar thing with the mind, supplanting distracting thoughts and images for the anxious ones, and allowing you to push the buttons on the remote control to shift your thoughts. These actions, to some degree anyway, do shift ones thoughts. And that's certainly an important degree, because both TV and food point to one's ability to actually influence, if not choose, different physical and mental states. And when you are really upset, having these ways of calming or distracting can be very helpful.

But where these coping strategies become unhelpful is when we reach after such coping devices from a place of desperation, not from a place of choice.

For instance, Sandy used a lot of coffee to manage her anxiety, without fully realizing what its purpose was. If asked, she'd say, "Well, I just like coffee." In therapy, when we explored what it might be like to diminish her intake, she noticed a lot of fear arising. She was afraid that she would fall apart in her day-to-day life if she changed how much coffee she drank. But, in realizing the purpose of coffee, she was able to start experimenting with factors like how much she drank, and when during the day she drank it, even abstaining at times. Ultimately, she was able to use coffee strategically for those days when the anxiety was too strong to manage with her other skills, or when she needed to get worldly stuff accomplished and couldn't dedicate the time to meditating or investigating the details of the anxiety.

Anxiety has much to do, at the level of thought, with feeling out of control, and Sandy's learning was that she could both get the suppressant effects of coffee as needed, but also could feel more in control of the process, of when she chose to drink caffeine, rather than letting the choice be habitual and maybe even a misreading of what she really needed.

Because within anxiety is a message about something lacking, either as a "psychic nutrient," or as a desire. Often within her anxiety was a feeling of wanting to feel more competent (not just, notice, feeling incompetent, but having an active desire), and when she stumbled on an activity that made her feel that, her anxiety reduced or dissipated. In other words, there was information in the anxiety, not just, as it were, stupid neurons.

So our work focused for a time on making a practice of asking herself, "What do I need in this moment?" and then really listening. Often the first response would be a knee-jerk, "It doesn't matter because I can't change anything anyway!" But we worked to recognize this voice of disempowerment, and to listen *past it* to the intuitive place in her that could give her a real answer. Her answer was often, "It would help if I felt more effective," which the TV and overeating and coffee actually never satisfied, often making her feel *more* incompetent. These coping strategies were surrogates for empowerment which never really satisfied, because these feelings were never the real thing.

We are always faced with a choice when our moods become wild, but without being able to connect to the wisdom within us, we don't act self-destructively as much as we act on poor information. So Sandy had to learn to tolerate, and *practice* tolerating, that unformed space between "I can't!" and the wisdom that would eventually arise, and then to act on that wisdom to help herself get what her system was lacking.

I say "system" intentionally, because what was so important was to shift from the sense of personal endangerment that fueled the anxiety, to a more neutral, experimental stance of examining her need and then, as if designing her own diet, added the missing nutrients and noticing the results.  The control that is arrived at is an authentic one based in observation and direct response to our real needs, not in an image of control (like frantically pushing buttons on the remote console) which is ultimately unstable and ineffective.

What Sandy learned was that even within the storm of anxiety, there was a place of calm from which she could assess her need, and that over time, in practicing responding to her own wisdom about her needs, she could actually shift her mood.  In learning not to struggle *against* anxiety, but to move *with*, it like boating through rapids, she could actually diminish the mood and build up a grounded faith in her ability to get out of the whirlpool of anxiety.  The voice of helplessness and powerlessness came to sound a bit tinny when it arrived, because she remembered more and more often past times of finding what she genuinely needed.

And finally, at a deeper level, she began to trust that she actually could provide what she, in moments, lacked, and that life apparently was not a desert, but rather a buffet table on which she could find the experiences that she *actually* needed.

## ESSAY 10: FILTERING OUR WORLDS, FOR GOOD AND WILL

When I first arrived in San Francisco from a much smaller town, the stimuli of just driving around the city was near overwhelming. Cars, bikes, scooters, pedestrians, pedestrians with dogs, dog walkers with packs of dogs, stop lights, honking horns, roads built for carriages, blinking signs, beautiful buildings, stunning views—my mind was hyperventilating with what to pay attention too.

Life, we can agree, offers us a tremendous amount of data. If we were to pay attention to all of it, equally, we'd be lost in an ocean of signals and stimulation. What keeps this from happening is brain's automatic filtering of this data. There are different types of filters—like how the eye filters for color, the body for hot and cold, or the mind for danger—but all act to make order out of the buzzing confusion of life.

As with the external stimulus, the mind is always making decisions about what internal data is important or not, interesting or not, dangerous or not—those questions determine what the mind gives attention and "mental space" to, and what is ignored. The whole body, the whole conglomerate of trillions and trillions of cells, is constantly communicating with itself, between cells, between brain cells, between organs, between the mind and the body. Electrical, chemical, mechanical, hydraulic—huge amounts of signaling goes on. So what does the mind pay attention to?

You can see how there is a tremendous amount of filtering that goes on out of our conscious awareness, as there has to be. Thankfully, we don't have to choose moment by moment whether to think about signaling the white blood cells to take on that flu, or choose how to regulate our internal temperature.

Certain habits are just fine, thank you.

Yet there are very important (especially to sufferers of the wild moods) choices to be made in terms of where to consciously place our attention, choices that determine in large part what mood gets brought to fore, or sent to the back of our minds.

For instance, when you are exercising, what is the relevant information to pay attention to? And how do you know? When you hear the thought, "Stop, this is too painful!" where is it actually coming from? When you feel the tension in your calves, running on the treadmill, is that a sign of impending cramp, or a good healthy work out?

Or, when you are feeling anxiety, and your heart speeds up, is that an imminent heart attack? Are you nearing your death? Is it a signal that your body is revving up to deal with a potential danger? What does it mean?

Noam Chomsky, the linguist and political writer, has said that people are essentially rational, but that they are fed poor data: essentially, with "bad data" we get "bad results." In Buddhist terms, we are misperceiving, misinterpreting reality, and then acting on that ignorance (that false model of reality), which produces suffering. Chomsky has focused on the bad information coming from mass media and how that affects public discourse and opinion, but for the wild moods, the more salient place to look is how we are telling ourselves bad stories, selecting for ourselves the distorted information, and then believing the resulting narrative.

Which begs the question, how do we make more accurate stories from our outer and inner data? I think the answer really boils down to: breathe, and be curious. With the panic attack example, it's being mindful of the experience, the data—racing heart, temple throbbing, fear—in a curious, interested way. "Hmm, what is this?" is the essential attitude. Inquisitiveness and curiosity. With this mindset, the "real," or more accurate, less filtered version of reality comes to the fore, because we are not, as it were, forcing the light through any number of prisms.

If I'm running on the treadmill and the thought comes that I *have* to stop, I can question it: "Is that true?" And then see what comes with that openness.

Which requires a certain stability, in terms of focus and emotions, but that all can be developed with work and attention.

Which is not to say any of this is easy, because there are reasons why we've learned to filter for certain information (usually "negative data"). Yet we can learn to be more objective in interpreting our own data, our own signals, from heart, mind, body, and spirit. We learn to allow in the data and sitting with it to allow the order and meaning already there to emerge, without forcing a judgment out of fear.

# ESSAY 11: THE INTOLERABLES

Why is it that in some areas of our lives, it's no problem, we flow around obstacles like a cork on a river, and other areas, we are an iron anchor? Why do we get stuck? And why do we get stuck, *where* we get stuck?

In my work with couples, we talk about "The Intolerables," those places where we dig in our heels and just refuse to budge. With one person, their Intolerable might be around their partner's messiness. Another, around not getting a certain amount of sex or intimacy. A third, not having enough time alone. The Intolerables are not just preferences, which are simply statements of desire; instead, they are conditions in the world (relationship, career, mood states, etc.) which, for a particular individual, simply *must* be met.

What these reactions are will vary from person to person, but they are all defensive. One couple I worked with, when the husband pushed too hard for his opinion to be heard, his wife tipped over her level of tolerance and snapped shut emotionally, often withdrawing to her study for a whole day. With another couple, the man, when asked for emotional contact, would space out and become unreachable.

Preference implies a certain flexibility: I'd like to go to the museum, but there are other things we could do that would also be OK. But intolerance implies a line in the sand: cross this mark and there are dire consequences. "I'll go this far and no farther," is the voice of intolerance.

So, if the Intolerables are demarcated by a (relatively) sudden drop into defensiveness...what then is being defended? Take a minute to check in around one of your Intolerables. What marks the edge of your tolerance, and what happens when you reach it? What are you feeling as you go over that edge? What are you thinking; or, what story are you telling yourself about the situation, such that you feel you need to go into a defensive posture? (And here, attack is seen as the more active form of defending.)

In my experience, the Intolerables boil down to those areas where we feel our self is being threatened in a profound way. This isn't a sticks and stones situation; these "thou shalt nots" are about life and death, about our survival.

The defenses of the self, the guards on the castle walls who are charged with the survival of the kingdom, react when the alarm bell rings, when the self seems under attack. The type of reaction—retreating, attacking, pulling up the drawbridge, going invisible, any of the myriad ways of defending—is determined by a person's character and past history, as is the conditions under which the alarm goes off.

So, as an example, Sarah grew up with an alcoholic father who was normally withdrawn, but who could fly into violent rages at unpredictable times. She could handle her husband's irritation OK, but when he ramped up to anger, it crossed a line for her and she would start stonewalling, withdrawing emotionally more and more until she threatened divorce. Even if he was owning his anger, and voicing it appropriately, for her it triggered memories that made her feel profoundly threatened. (Which means at a neurological level, that her system was being activated in a similar way to when she *actually* was faced with a rageful father—i.e., there's something very real being re-experienced.)

Or take Ben, whose mother was depressed and unavailable emotionally for most of his early years. With his wife, who had a tendency towards depression, he could take about a week of her gloomy moods. But after that, he would feel less and less tolerant and sympathetic, and quickly move towards despair and thoughts of how his wife didn't love or care about him. At two weeks, he would start entertaining ideas of leaving (this option of "radical separation" almost always goes along with one's Intolerables).

So what are the solutions?

There's two ways to go with the Intolerables: management, making the situation conform to these "requirements"; or, letting go of the "requirements."

Now, the first we're all pretty familiar with. You could probably do a full assessment of your successes and failures in these terms: what are my Intolerables, and how have I designed my life and relationships to conform to them? And there's a lot to be said for being able to get one's needs met in the world, no doubt about that. The problem with the Intolerables, though, comes from the rigidity of reaction to what is perceived as "not to be tolerated."

For most people, the "letting go" response to the Intolerables is much less familiar, almost by definition: we are loathe to let go of what seems to protect our survival. But, to my mind, this "letting go" approach is what actually makes any system—whether a relationship to others, or to life in general, or to one's own moods of depression and anxiety—more flexible and resilient.

This approach to the Intolerables is the harder, but ultimately more rewarding path. The Intolerables are markers of where we believe we cannot survive reality, and since reality (in the form of the facts of relationship, that our wife is actually not interested in doing the dishes, really) always, in the end, defeats our wins, these places are sites of deep suffering. In fighting for the maintenance of our "selves," our self definitions, we are like brick walls in the surf. The ocean doesn't stop, and our rigidity in meeting the endless waves means we are pounded by the inevitable over and over...and over...

To learn that we can actually survive what now feels intolerable is, ironically, to allow ourselves (actually, "our selves") to be broken. Meaning, to resist the urge to defend, to stay present to the reality (our wife's withdrawal, our husband's anger, our own depression), keeping engaged, and asking, "Have I been destroyed?"

The trick, though, is to ask the question without then jumping to trying to answer it. You toss it out there and then just look, staying in that questioning space. As if it were less a question and more of a prayer, open and without panic.

What you'll notice in doing this is that, because the question (if you stay with the openness long enough, not collapsing into defensiveness, contraction) of "Have I been destroyed" is seen as a simple, "No," then there's a fundamental change. "Intolerable" turns into "preference." You'd prefer your husband not be angry—it's annoying and takes energy to deal with—but you know deep down it's not a matter of life and death.

# ESSAY 12: SEEING THROUGH YOUR "INTOLERABLES"

I wrote a while back about "The Intolerables," those places in our selves where we say, "Hell or high water, this shall not stand!" Now, there is much to be said about setting our boundaries firmly and clearly, and to responding directly to what we deem is unjust. And there is much to be said for a strong will. However, what I've noticed is that often, in declaring our Intolerables, we are attempting to solve problems that may, ultimately, be unsolvable (or at least unsolvable in the *way* we think they have to be solved).

For instance, let's say Joe's Intolerable is that he will *never* clean up after his wife. Never, in no circumstance, ever, for any reason. It has caused many fights, this principled position (she calls it "rigid and stubborn"), but he will not budge. It is "intolerable" for him to imagine playing the role of "maid" to his wife, and her protestations only make him more entrenched.

Now, what problem is Joe trying to solve? Let's say in his family of origin, he was the second oldest of nine kids, and while the eldest got to be the star athlete, Joe was made to be the supervisor of his siblings. At some point he rebelled, and has been rebelling ever since against that (imposed) role.

The problem he is trying to solve is the *feeling* of being mistreated and overwhelmed with responsibility or work that he believes is not his to do, that is being imposed on him. When this feeling arises—his wife is running late and needs him to take care of the dishes—he starts to become flooded with memories and feelings (rage, impotence, grief) that were exactly what he experienced as a child but had no way to express. So he's developed his Intolerable as a way of suppressing the re-experiencing of all that pain. "I'm *not* going to do your dishes" is his way of saying, "You won't make me feel like I used to feel, because now I have some control."

Which is totally understandable, and if we look, we can make a list of our own Intolerables. It's a universal tendency in humans to defend against overwhelm, and the "I shall not!" stands are one way of defending.

And...they don't work. The emotions we're keeping at bay with our rigid stance don't actually resolve by being suppressed. And when we keep holding others responsible for being the cause of our suffering ("If my wife did the dishes, I would never feel like this!"), we have to maintain a defensive, hardened stance to "hold them off." In other words, at a subtle or not so subtle level, we are constantly feeling, or anticipating being, attacked.

So if the Intolerables don't, ultimately, work, what does? If you go through a process of examining what is the root of the Intolerable, you come to see that in terms of solving the "problem" (Joe's desire not to *feel* controlled), other people and their actions or inactions are, well, they're simply not relevant.

This understanding of the "irrelevance" of other's actions is actually the insight that arises when an Intolerable (a rigid position/stance) is very near to resolution. What was a problem to be heroically solved through battle is not actually "solved," but rather the "problem" itself is dissolved. Joe comes to realize that his wife's messiness is utterly irrelevant to whether or not he has to defend against his *feelings* of being controlled, and that the control he's trying to get through refusing his wife's demands is better found by addressing the root cause, because his wife is not *ultimately* the problem.

Control, he comes to realize, is about allowing his feelings to happen and learning to understand where they came from, and how they keep playing out and shaping his present life (like with his wife). In other words, to spot the internal feelings as separate from what triggers them (wife!), and realize that if those feelings are managed and made sense of, the dishes in the sink become irrelevant. The "problem" all along was the *feeling* of being controlled, and when he learns to relate to ("control" in the best sense) his feelings differently, then the conflict with his wife disappears.

This experience of recognizing this irrelevance, though, is not at all depressing or tragic, nor is it usually felt as a big liberating relief. It's more of a simple thought (at its clearest), as an insight without the fireworks. "Oh, it doesn't actually matter. What I thought was the point...isn't." And then you go on, *free to make choices*, rather than having your choice already made by your Intolerable.

# ESSAY 13: THE MOOSEHEAD GIFTS

Here are some thoughts about the "moose head gifts" that life brings us...frequently. You know, those experiences that come along, that seem to fit into our lives about as well as that stuffed moose head that our uncle once gave us. Getting fired unexpectedly. Car wrecks. Losses. Physical illness. All the things that we not only don't want, but believe, deep down, that we cannot survive if and when they happen.

These are the gifts, though, that when we really sit down and thoroughly unwrap them, what we find inside are forgotten parts of ourselves.

I've picked up one of the philosopher Ken Wilber's early books, called *No Boundary*, which is a discussion of the different ways in which we as humans construct, or divide, our sense of self. Starting from the relative diffuseness of a newborn's consciousness, we go about the process of defining our *self*, inscribing what's within the definition of self, and what's experienced as foreign and "other." Wilber's divisions are:

- Persona level: an individual's persona (our "social face") is self, and their unwanted mental bits (shadow) are "other"
- Ego level: the ego is self, and the body is seen as "other"
- Total organism: the body-mind is self, and the environment is "other"
- Unity Consciousness: all experience/phenomena is seen as self, and therefore there's no "other"

Far from being esoteric, these splits are the stuff of our day-to-day lives. Look for those areas where you perpetually do battle or experience conflict, and that will mark the border of self and other. These splits are especially perceptible in our relationships, where to a large degree we partner up with those parts of ourselves (in our "significant other") which we haven't (yet) been able to recognize as *ours*.

The way in which we arrange the particular fences that define the property lines of our Self comes in large part from the way the world, especially our parents/caregivers, mirror back to us the acceptable vs. the unacceptable parts of the self. For instance, if parents are natural and laid back about an infant's various body fluids, then that child is not taking in the message that there's something undesirable about the natural body. He or she will grow up (barring other factors) with a sense that body functions are just natural, no big deal in the scheme of things (the original scheme of things being their parents). There's more of a willingness to see body *as* self, rather than if the opposite messages were given, that the body is somehow "wrong." In that case, one tends to distance from identifying with body because in a subtle or not-so-subtle way, body is shown to be dangerous, and that danger is that the vicissitudes of body scared the parents. When you as infant are totally dependent on your parents for food and emotional nurturing, then if your body seems to cause your emotional or literal connection with your parents to waver, you will learn to deny your body because, literally, an infant depends on emotional sustenance as much as on food.

The same is true for the other splits, in terms of the received messages about: the dangerousness/desirability of parts of the psyche (say, anger or love); the environment (other cultures/people, the messy natural world); or spiritual realms (our deeper unities with the world and others).

But the upshot is that where there are splits in our psyche—as understandable and worthy of empathy are their origins—there is suffering. Why? Because we are cutting ourselves off from our own selves, constantly ostracizing ourselves from the full community that at some level we *know* we belong to. We are repeatedly *dis-membering* our Self.

There's no blame or shame in this, though, because it's simply what humans *do*. And one can say that the developmental path of growth is a path of remembering that what's on the other side of the fence is not just something we're *related* to, but something that we really (and truly) *are*.

So the "moosehead gifts" of life, if we are truly, at essence, an un-bounded oneness, are really just parts of ourselves that we've learned to disown. The experiences we don't want—whether the irritation of our partner's messiness, or the pain of losing a parent, or the fear of experiences of unbounded spaciousness—show us those places where we are divided. The "bad mate," the "depriving world," the "horrid emptiness," they are all parts or experiences of ourselves which we've learned to spurn and resist.

This is why intimate relationships are such wonderful, painful places of learning. The annoying habits of our partners are actually the lost bits of ourselves; they bring us gifts of their "noxious" bits, but if we actually open these packages, what we find is the box is full of parts of ourselves. The unkemptness of our partner, that we reject and abhor, is actually carrying their wisdom about, say, a way of being which does not pressure our environment to be orderly. We may choose not to adopt the *form* of that ease—I, for instance, simply work better when my tool bench is organized— but the opportunity is there to find the quality of ease in ourselves which has been lost or disowned.

What I've seen in the act of reclaiming these "moosehead" parts of our self, healing these splits, is not really an experience of heroic triumph, but rather of familiar affection and recognition. For instance, when talking about his first deep-water scuba dive, my friend described it as, given how much fear he'd had, "oddly familiar." He said, "There were all the usual elements, just with a lot of water. And the critters were just doing what all critters do. Eating, fighting, relating, running away—all things I do too." In other words, he recognized the elements of the ocean as the same constituent elements of himself.

You know when you've bridged this gap of otherness because you drop into peace and relaxation. The guards on the walls of your self recognize their fellows, and with a "Traveler, well met!", open the gates and either look over other chasms for danger, or at the end of the journey, see that there's really no danger against which they need to defend.

# ESSAY 14: RE-MEMBERING

Let's start from the idea that every individual has the capacity for all the mood states, from bleak depression and runaway anxiety, to elation and joy, and that the differences among people in terms of mood is not their capacity but their "habits." If it were a question of capacity, then presumably people suffering from, say, chronic depression, would never have felt anything but depression, and would never have any reprieves, any light days or happy moments. So if that's true, then what we've got is a problem of *remembering*.

Laurel Parnell, a psychologist and specialist in EMDR (Eye Movement Desensitization and Reprocessing), has written a book called *Tapping In*, about the use of what she calls "resource tapping." Resource tapping uses the central discovery of EMDR, that when the brain is stimulated *bi-laterally* (by either moving the eyes back and forth, or tapping sequentially on each side of the body, or use of audio pulses), and traumatic memory is held in the mind, then there is a discharge or release of the trauma. It's a rather odd discovery that was made in the late 80's, and the scientists have not quite figured it out theoretically, but it does work and the research data shows that it is effective in relieving the symptoms of trauma.

However, Parnell's book is about how, when positive thoughts are held in the mind, and then bi-lateral stimulation is applied, those thoughts become more *seated*, like gently tapping on a peg to seat it in its hole. The thought (usually as an image) is brought to mind to evoke a desired feeling (say, safety), and when that desired sense is felt in the body, the tapping is applied.

As an example, I was working with a woman who felt frightened a lot. I asked her to think of a person or animal who, when brought to mind, carried a sense of protection and caring for her. She thought about it, and after a little bit, the image of a lizard came to mind. She'd been very connected to lizards as a child, living on a farm and on the edge of a large forest, where these animals had given her solace in a fairly lonely upbringing. She called the lizard forth, and she tapped on her knees, "tapping it in," allowing the associated sense of safety to strengthen.

She wasn't at all sure anything had happened when she left the session, though the lizard image had been consoling in the moment. But the next time we met, she told me that she'd been walking down a street near her house, and a car had almost run her down in a crosswalk. Whereas typically she would have shot into a panic and stayed there for some time, what she noticed was that immediately the image of the lizard sprang to mind, and in her imagination began stroking her hair like a mother with her child. She saw that her system began calming down right away, and she did not carry the fright beyond the incident itself. What could have been a low-grade trauma (an overwhelm of her nervous system) was simply a jet of adrenalin.

As you can see, she did not try consciously to soothe herself. The work we did created an association between feeling frightened and the soothing image of the lizard was such that when the emotion arose, the soothing also happened. Through this image an equilibrium was reestablished and trauma avoided. (And to note: which image is used is actually quite arbitrary. The content is only important in that a particular individual's "system" associates the image with the desired feeling/state.)

What's happening is that resources that are *already* there in an individual are being accessed and connected with other parts of the mind/brain. My client had the *capacity* for self-soothing, but just wasn't remembering how or when to do it. Her problem wasn't a resource problem, it was a remembering problem.

My preference, though, is for the term *re-membering*, as it seems to me a little more evocative and accurate. Our psyche's inevitably become *dis-membered* throughout our lives, often most strongly in our childhoods (via belief systems or trauma), and our natural resources go dormant, becoming relatively unused or unaccessed. With depression, say, states of peace and self-acceptance don't disintegrate or die, they simply become disassociated from the individual. The depressed person, in a deep way, *forgets* that they have this capacity to experience, well, un-depression, and it requires effort and practice to remember the capacities exist, and then to *re-member* the psyche so that these resources become more readily available to day-to-day life.

The wonderful thing, though, is that with most people, their forgotten resources are just in the penumbra of consciousness, and can often be quickly called in. I've seen people who are cycling in fear or anxiety find images that, whoosh!, connect them to a state of safety so quickly it initially surprised me (and them!). Depression sometimes is a bit more difficult; the resources are there, but instead of being in the next room, they might be downstairs in the basement. However, these resources do exist, and with other supports (medication, nutrition, exercise, more social contact) these resources become easily available as well.

The other wonderful thing about this resource work is that the resources that a person finds are unequivocally theirs. My client's lizard image came from within her own brain, and the soothing that ensued also came from own brain and neurological system. So if that's where it arose (and not from some outside intervention, divine or medical), and she's presumably always walking around with her own brain, then the resource is potentially *always available*.

Then it's just a matter of remembering.

# ESSAY 15: BELIEFS AND THE LIMITS
# OF WORK SATISFACTION

Martin Seligman, the founder of Positive Psychology, takes up the question (in his book, <u>Authentic Happiness</u>) of what makes the same employment for one person utter drudgery, and for another, a passionate pursuit. It is a question that bears on those who struggle with depression and/or anxiety, not because finding the right job will be the cure-all, but because satisfying work is a prophylactic against wild moods. Working with these moods, in some ways, is like erecting breakwaters in a harbor: the waves don't stop, but by the time they roll in to your boat, they are relatively docile. Job choice is like one of the wave-tamers.

So what does Seligman say? From his and others' research, he makes a division between three types of employment:

1) Job: employment which serves primarily to support your non-job life (the office worker who plays in a band at night).

2) Career: employment which is enjoyable, but which is more about advancement and promotion than the work itself.

3) Calling: employment which in and of itself is satisfying and enjoyable, which is an integral part of the person's identity and sense of purpose in the world. This is work which is loved, and which is felt to make the world a better place.

The difference between a job or career and a calling is that a calling must engage your "signature strengths," those qualities which are most central to your character, to what you are good at doing, love to do, and which bring you deep satisfaction when deployed. A calling is work that repeatedly and routinely supplies gratification because it calls on your most important values and strengths.

It's a pretty simple idea, really: assess your signature strengths, and then choose work that fits those strengths, or take the job you're in and craft it to emphasize your strengths. So why, then, are so many people unsatisfied with their work?

One reason might be simple availability, that appropriate work is not available to you. Or your job will not bend or shift to accentuate your strengths. Or you don't know what your strengths actually are.

But what I've seen with depression and anxiety is that much more often it's not these "inhibitors" which are the trouble, but what is going on under the surface, in terms of a person's *belief's* about work and satisfaction. If there were nothing standing between knowing your strengths and acting on them, then voila! A calling! But what usually stands between is a belief that either "Life can't provide," or "I'm not worthy."

Beliefs, as I'm talking about them here, are not simple, neutral assessments, like "I believe it will rain today." That's probably more accurately stated as, "I think it's likely to rain." If it doesn't, you shrug and go on.

The beliefs that are problematic are those that emphasize your self as the believer: *I* believe x. In other words, these beliefs are statements or axioms about your *self*, or your *self in the world*. Whether it rains or not, no big deal in terms of how you see yourself. But a conception of the nature of yourself and the world, on which you base your self, stability, and meaning—that's a big deal.

We are wired as humans to maintain consistency in our sense of ourselves. Have you ever had a moment when you can't quite remember yourself clearly, maybe waking from a deep sleep? It's most often disorienting and even scary, and these reactions point to a deep part of ourselves that wants to always know who and where we are. Beliefs are part of this way of "locating" ourselves.

Think of guards on a castle wall, who are charged with the defense of the castle. That's their sole and only job. They don't care what is actually inside the castle, and once something is let through the gate, it simply becomes part of "the castle," what they defend. A tyrant, or a town council, or a goat, or a pile of garbage—doesn't matter at all to the guards.

So, too, with beliefs. The guards which patrol around the perimeter of our selves will equally defend what's inside against challenges, regardless of whether the castle (our self) holds thoughts of "I'm lovable and worthy," or "I'm terrible and worthless and the world is dangerous." The guards always face outward.

Regarding work life, the way this applies is: safety most often trumps satisfaction, and safety means defending the self (the castle) against challenge. If your core belief is that you do not deserve a calling, and your boss comes to you asking, "How can we draw on your core strengths?" you're likely to, in subtle or not so subtle ways, resist the opportunity. While the longing is surely there to grow and be happy—this is also a genuine force in the psyche—the danger to the stability of the self often wins out. Outwardly, it's, "Great!" and inwardly, it's, "If I take the opportunity, become happier, then my core belief about my self is disproved, and then who am I?" Fear arises, which alerts the guards, and then the castle goes into lock down.

This is the great dilemma of the wild moods, that they often serve to defend the self, such that the direct path—here, matching strengths with work—can become quite twisted. (Not, however, to discount genetics or chemistry—there are many factors at work in moods.)

The great solutions to the great dilemma, I'll talk about in other essays in this collection, but for now, just paying attention to this need to defend beliefs can be opening. You can ask yourself what exactly these beliefs are for you, and how you are defending them at work (or home, relationships, etc.). Awareness of what is going on is the critical work in changing course and, as it were, giving new orders to the guards up on your wall.

Because these guards are, ultimately, servants, important ones without whom your self would melt and blur or be taken over by others. But they can be retrained, and made to understood that the old, outdated threats are over and that certain experiences—like satisfaction at work—can now be let in without destroying the castle (one's self). Once the guards get a convincing briefing, they will happily go back to their posts and go about their same business, but the results for you are that they will allow through experiences that heretofore felt profoundly dangerous.

And once these guards are at ease, inasmuch as they have been keeping out more satisfying work, you will find that moving from job to career to calling becomes much more obvious and direct. These guards—they're basically good folk, they just need some guidance.

# ESSAY 16: THE RAW CREATIVTY OF DEPRESSION AND ANXIETY

You can look at working with depression and anxiety in two basic ways:

1) Management strategies: These strategies consist of such things as analyzing triggering thoughts, challenging the reality of pessimistic thinking, engaging in exercise, prayer, being with friends, etc., efforts gauged to "shrink" the mood to a manageable size. "Overwhelmed" literally means "to be covered over," as if your head were submerged in water. Management tools are about draining the water so you're not "covered over." Or another way of thinking about it is that you are shifting something from that which you are existing *in*, to something that is existing *in you*.

2) Transformational strategies: here you are also seeking to deal with the overwhelming quality of the mood, but instead of shrinking the mood to fit *within you*, you are expanding your self to *encompass the mood*. In other words, instead of working on the "size" of the mood (with the management strategies) you are working on the "size" of yourself.

It's the second strategy that I'm going to address here, and specifically one form of acceptance that can have a remarkable effect on your experience of wild moods. To warn you, it might seem a little weird or off-putting...or weird. And if it leaves you cold, then just set it aside like you might, well, how about a Durian, which for me is a perfectly legitimate fruit, just really hard to like. If this is your Durian, then just put it back on the shelf and move on. But taste it a little first...

So here's what I'm proposing that you try: see if you can find a real and genuine appreciation for the raw creativity of your depression and anxiety. With this, you're not trying to change anything, or struggle against the overwhelm. Don't attempt to drain the swamp or heave yourself onto shore. Just sit with the mood and see if you can experience it with an artist's eye, for the aesthetic richness of the mood itself.

One way to do this: imagine you are sitting in a theater, watching your life being performed up on stage. You are not in the play, just sitting back and seeing it happening. Remember that the backdrop to the play is a blank stage, just wood flooring and a curtain. That's what was there before the characters arrived, and after the drama is over, that's what will be left. So, with that in mind, let the content of the play—the specific characters saying their specific lines—drop into the background, and appreciate that there is *something* onstage rather than *nothing*. This is the effort to find that place in you that can relish the play *as a creative act*, a collecting of raw elements developing into forms and stories, movements and direction.

There is a part of all of us which delights in creativity just for its own sake, regardless of whether it's in the form of a comedy, tragedy, drama, Noh play, whatever. To the part of us which is invested in our story and its protagonist (Me!), this act of savoring of this creativity is something of an affront. From the "Me's" perspective, it can feel like an invalidation or disregard of the "Me's" suffering.

But from the "aficionado's" perspective, it's all just wonderful performance, and this perspective can be very valuable. Why? Because from this perspective, you can experience not having to struggle. You don't change the depression/anxiety, you shift your relationship, from onstage to the audience. This is one of the transformational strategies, because what's changing, in effect, not the mood, but *you*.

It is as if you're sitting in the front row of a movie theater. Management strategies are about shrinking the size of the screen till it's the size of a television set. Transformational strategies are about moving yourself to the back row of the theater.

The long term effects of both are actually different: management strategies manage overwhelm in the short-term; while transformational strategies create more profound changes by letting you experience the wild moods in deeper ways. When you see the moods from different angles, your *reactions* to them change, and thus the whole game changes.

With this "wild creativity" experiment, feel the difference between seeing your experience of depression and anxiety as an oppressive and inescapable force, versus seeing these emotions as an expression of an amazing, universal, raw force of creation. What happens if and when your perspective shifts?

But, as I said earlier, if this is a "Durian" to you, give it back to the fruit seller and move on to whatever is tastier.

# ESSAY 17: MINDFULNESS AND CHOICE

A friend recently told me about a meditation retreat he'd worked on while traveling in India. On these retreats, you are either participating as a meditator, teacher, or worker—he was the latter, helping cook and clean and do odd jobs. "Which may seem easier than sitting," he said, "but, pfew, stuff was coming up!"

He described how, mid-way through the course, he began having overwhelming cravings for sweets. He would go in the kitchen between sittings, grab a roll of the English tea cookies, dip them in black tea chai, and then roll that in course ground sugar. The resulting "food" items were then eaten one after another.

"I went to the teacher on the retreat and said, 'Look, I'm having all these problems with food, and I'm afraid to go in the kitchen, but I can't keep away. What should I do?'"

His teacher replied, "Well, when you go in the kitchen to work, if you find yourself having to have one of these cookies, simply be *mindful* when you eat it. Pay attention to what it feels like to lift the cookie, to dip it, to chew it, the whole process. *Observe it.* You'll be fine."

My friend, wanting to *do* something, was non-plussed, but without any other solution, tried it out. He paid close attention to the lifting, to the dipping, to the rolling, to the chewing, to the swallowing, observing it as objectively as he could in the moment, attempting to avoid the struggle or doing modes.

"After the first half-dozen cookies, I noticed the craving began to wane. Part of me was just looking at all this and wasn't even judgmental, just noted that this behavior wasn't good for me, and didn't solve the problem it was misguidedly intended to solve. The anxiety underlying the eating became obvious, and equally obvious was the fact that the sugar and caffeine-fest was not helping anything. After that, what cravings came up were noted by this observing part of myself and seen for what they were, a desire to tamp down the emotions."

"I didn't have to wrestle the demons to the ground and keep them pinned, I just had to see clearly that I wasn't acting in my best interest, and then it was as if I got—*really* got—that putting my hand on the stove was counter-productive. The desire just evaporated."

I love my friend's story, because it so clearly illustrates the principle that what we do that is not in our self-interest is done without our full awareness. When my friend brought awareness to his cookie eating, the reality of what was happening became clear. Reaching for a cookie, his mind no longer said, "I'm trying to survive!" but rather, "I'm avoiding facing the emotions which, if faced, would actually give me some peace." If he had just tried to argue the point with himself, then all he would have gotten would have been more tension. But the *experience* of his own resistance (the cookies) clarified the *reason* or *function* of the compulsive actions (wolfing down the cookies). In this clarification there arose choice, and once there was a choice of what do to about the strong emotions, then his mind naturally moved towards the healthier rather than the less healthy solutions. It's when we feel we don't have a real choice that we choose poorly.

For all our human foibles and confusions, there's a part of our mind which is blunt and direct and self-centered about choosing action: if it doesn't benefit us, choose something else. When the mind is exposed to the *clear experience* of error, it changes. Fighting is not necessary. Debate team cleverness is mostly useless. Only *experience* gets the fist to let go of the thorns.

I remember having a conversation with a different friend who was involved in a sort of politically motivated shop lifting habit. This person explained the thefts as a righteous and appropriate response to what she described as the rapacious behavior of corporate chain stores. But picking up on her agitation, I asked about the feelings involved. She became a bit stony, but because of her basic deep integrity, had to take a look. I said, "Next time you're stealing, pay attention to how it actually feels. Is it pleasant at base? Unpleasant? Are you agitated or relaxed? Does it feel like something good for you?"

She agreed to do this, and when we talked a bit after that conversation, she was a little chagrined to report that, no, at the level of feeling it was painful to steal, and when she really looked, it did not seem to be in her self-interest. The behavior was not wrestled away from her grasping hands; when exposed to awareness, she naturally let it drop. Our deepest self doesn't want to hold onto what's painful or useless, and when something is seen as such, despite or even in contradiction to our political stances, we find we're just unable to keep holding it.

You can probably see how this principle applies to the vicissitudes of anxiety and depression. A couple situations that come to my mind are:

- Knowing that exercise helps stabilize us when the depressive spiral begins, we nonetheless rationalize watching TV instead of taking a walk through the park.

- We're taking herbal or prescription medications for anxiety, and though there has been relief from the medication, find ourselves avoiding the morning dose because "I'm just too rushed."

- We find ourselves on the computer all night instead of sleeping, and wake tired and less effective at work, causing more stress and anxiety.

But instead of looking at what you're choosing to do and going into hyper-critical mode ("See, I'm worthless, I'll never get out of these moods!") or fight mode ("I have to kill these behaviors! I have to wrench them away from myself if I'm going to survive!"), you just observe the patterns. Watch the TV program, but do so consciously, mindfully. You might find that actually, if you watch for 30 minutes, it does actually help buoy your spirits. Or you could find that the TV shows make your depression worse exactly when you're trying to make it better. Same for the meds and not sleeping: just watch your behavior and choices carefully, and the reality of what's really good for you will arise to meet your awareness.

AND!...I know this isn't easy when a part of your mind and brain, the part that is charged with just keeping you safe at all costs, is screaming that "You have to DO something!" When you're looking for the lion in the grass, contemplating your behavior in a mindful way *itself* feels threatening.

So adopting this principle, that "nothing against one's self-interest can be done in the face of full awareness," is a process and practice, and when you are too overwhelmed to observe, so be it. That's where you are. Don't fight. Accept it and move on to the next moment. Practice your coping skills to come back to center, knowing that there's plenty of time to practice, and as you do, the principle will become more and more real and its usefulness will become obvious.

Ironically, at that point of development, the "Protector" part of your psyche begins to see that, actually, mindfulness seems to be safer, in the long run, then some of the habitual behaviors. The Protector then begins to loosen up and allow for observation more often, without being flooded with panic, which is the kind of upward spiral you want to be in.

## ESSAY 18: THE DEPRESSIVE SPIRAL

If you've experienced depression throughout your life, then you know what the depressive spiral feels like. There is something stressful that happens that sends you down, seemingly without being able to stop the descent. For instance, say you get upbraided by your boss for a small mistake. You initially feel anger, with the attached thought, "This is so unfair!" Then you feel powerless, and think, "But what can I do?" The physical deadening sensations creep in, and you think, "Oh, no, here it is again." The sense of powerlessness deepens, and then you get angry: "Why can't I control this? I hate that I can't do anything about this." The deadening gets even stronger, and you react more, to the original stimulus, plus the anger, plus the sensations, plus the self-criticism...

If there isn't something that you can do or that happens to anchor you, you'll sink down to a collapsed place, like a whirl pool at the bottom of a funnel. Then when you make your way back up to the surface, there's an added layer of fear about getting caught in that cycle again, often leading to avoidant behavior (maybe trying to be perfect at work, always please your boss, etc.).

As kids, we used to run around the inside wall of the three foot high Doughboy swimming pool, causing a whirlpool to form that got stronger the harder we pushed into the current. However, when we stopped and ran in the opposite direction, the current would lessen and then break up. In the same way, the energy of depression can be disrupted; one can learn to both break up the spiraling, as well as to drain off the energy (we never tried to punch a hole in the pool wall, but that would have also worked to stop the spiraling).

The breaking up of the spiral requires first noticing when you are actually *beginning* to spiral, and developing a faith, through effective action, that you can do something about it. These are the "coping skills," or management strategies of living with depression. You might, for instance, notice yourself getting panicky about the work situation, but instead of believing the voice of that panic ("I'm powerless and in danger of losing my job...but I have to do something!"), you slow down and question your thinking. This is running against the current in order not to feed its energy. If you, without reflection, accept that it is the right time to panic, then you are swimming with the depression current and, like in the Doughboy, making it stronger.

This slowing down and paying attention (and questioning the voice of depression) is a big strategy in not feeding your energy into the depression, regardless of what *specifically* you do when you slow down (e.g., challenging your thoughts, getting exercise, getting support from a friend, etc.).

So: these coping skills are the "doing," active part of disrupting the spiral, while mindfulness practice is the "being" strategy that leads to the dissipation of the spiral of depression ("mindfulness" being the intentional, non-judgmental observation of the present experience). Mindfulness practice is climbing out of the pool altogether and letting the current gently fade out, because depression needs to be fed to continue. Like anything else that goes unfed, it eventually dissipates all by itself.

What, then, actually drives this spiral? One of the major "pushes" is the mind's tendency towards *rumination*. As the authors of The Mindful Way through Depression write, "When we ruminate, we become fruitlessly occupied with the fact that we are unhappy and with the causes, meanings, and consequences of our unhappiness." We try to solve the emotional problem of depression with the tool of cognition, and though it doesn't work, we continue this rumination because, essentially, we are convinced that thinking is the only way out of the unhappiness. But trying to control through thought, which is so useful in other realms and pursuits, doesn't work with emotions. You can build a bridge with that logical mindset, but try to have a relationship based on the same rules.

So the alternative to this "problem solving mind," what actually works with the emotions of depression, is mindfulness, acceptance of the present *as it is*, rather than continually comparing the present to the desired future, and finding oneself, one's life, and the world in generally constantly lacking. (And this is not opposed to action, because from this acceptance options are clarified, and effective actions can unfold.)

Depression feeds on this perceived deficiency, whereas mindfulness practice opens us up to, not the *idea* of plenty, but the actual experience that in this very moment, there is nothing wrong, and that the world is full of options and possibilities. As you develop this capacity to observe, the experiences of this "ok-ness" deepens, and it starts automatically undercutting despair. (You can still see what you want to change, but it doesn't wrench you emotionally.)

You'll find yourself running with the depression, pushing it along, and then, without even trying, you'll remember, "Oh, I *really* don't have to do this!" and either push back or get out of the pool

You will fall back in, of course, but with an ongoing mindfulness practice, you stay in less and less, get submerged more infrequently, and stop swimming so hard with the spiral.

# ESSAY 19: THE NEED FOR PRACTICE

As a bright but shy kid, I can remember many times when some insight into a problematic aspect of myself was perfectly clear, but how to fix it was totally baffling. The problem was clear, but clear like tropical fish under a glass-bottomed boat. You can see the fish in all their shapes and colors, but you can't touch them, you can't interact in any effective way and so you're just left to watch the problems continually do their thing.

Depression and anxiety can feel like that (especially if your mind runs towards the left brain, analytic side of things): you know the problem—you can see it right there under the glass—but the solution seems totally inaccessible.

So, here's my proposition: the *solution* to this lack of efficacy lies in practice, in learning through doing.

In taking ones self-understanding as one's map, and then exercises as the driving—not in the sense of carrying around your workbook all the time, in a formal and mechanical studiousness, but in the sense that you approach your moments as experiences that have something to teach you. Not "teach" as in, say, memorizing the periodic table, but learning as in how to improve your tennis serve. It's a muscular learning, a little change in what you *know*, and a big change in what you *do*.

Depression and anxiety are, quite literally, habits. They are often unconscious ways that both the mind *and* the body collaborate to create these wild moods. Which is not to discount all the research on the genetic and neurological roots of these moods (or mood states), but the concept of "habit" can, I think, apply to these aspects of depression and anxiety. Medications can be looked at as one way in which the "habits" of the body can be changed, exercise another, etc. (How about this: habits are repeating patterns, conscious or unconscious, that can be changed.)

So, deep learning does not happen as a result of just gaining knowledge, but happens because we have different *experiences* that change basic ways of responding to our world. If we see a rattlesnake in the road in front of us, the danger circuits in our brain will turn on, our heart rate will go up, our attention will narrow (we're probably not going to be planning dinner at this moment). But when we look closely and realize it's an artfully bent stick, that same deep part of our mind calms down, and it will not get agitated about that same stick again. The learning is both, "Oh, it's a stick," and the deeper part of the mind, "Oh, it's not a danger, I'll turn off the klaxon and shut down the defenses." The first is knowledge that facilitates the change in body state. But imagine if you flashed on what looks convincingly like a snake, and then had to stand there, eyes shut, while you repeated, "It's a stick, only a stick." You might flood yourself with the idea, but without being able to test it, visually, tactilely, your body isn't going to buy it.

There is, of course, real chemistry involved in depression and anxiety. It's not all about changes in insight and perception. Body-based interventions like medication are often very important in overcoming these moods, in changing physical and neurological set-points (or "habits"). But, in my experience, without intentional, mindful practice ("learning through doing"), a medication like Prozac manages symptoms without actually changing those habits that undergird the wild moods.

So, as psychotherapists, and many patients have realized over the years, "insight is not enough." An experimental, mindful approach to ones own suffering is the way to get down there in the water and catch some fish; this mindset both offers opportunities to learn, as well as being itself an experience of empowerment. Even if you're having trouble getting out of bed because of anxiety, you can still feel some control by experimenting with the anxiety. "What happens if I roll onto my stomach? What about opening the curtain a little? Does the anxiety increase or decrease? If I review my plans for the day, better or worse? Remember my nice lunch date yesterday, then what?" Following through on the experimental question will give you fresh information. "Oh! The curtains make me more anxious, but being on my stomach feels soothing. Huh!"

Experimental questions—that is, *practices*—like this can be created in any situation. Certainly it's tougher to scrape together the objectivity when you're under the weight of a runaway mood (there are definitely times to close the curtains and watch a B-movie), but even there you might be surprised at what you can do. Permanent changes in the *habits* of anxiety and depression are possible because, by offering the brain, body, and mind new, direct experiences of reality through experimentation, the brain, body, and mind learn that reality is different than the fear or hopelessness stories of these wild moods. They also learn to be active and self-directed; like doing curls in the gym will inevitably build your biceps, exercising with mood will inevitably build a similar strength and resilience. Despite what your head may think, the rest of you *will* actually change, and then your head gets to play catch up.

# ESSAY 20: PARENTS MATTER!

Psychotherapy, in the popular mind, is often described as a kind of navel-gazing exercise in "Blame the Parents." There certainly has been a fair share of thinking that one's adult problems and neuroses all begin with one's parents (less so now, but it's still around), but as someone recently put it, "That's way too simple."

Yet, it is true that what our parents did, or didn't do, affected us, helping to instill qualities and patterns that we play out in our adult lives. If your parents taught you (for instance) that business people can't be trusted, you're likely going to find yourself feeling anxious when you are around such folk (or maybe you compensate by becoming a super-ethical business person, just to show 'em).

Yet, with the work in the neurosciences and genetics—among other fields—it's gotten pretty clear that parents are not destiny. There is a space between what we have experienced, and what we are, and therefore, what we can do.

Then, how to reconcile the claims that parents are very important, and parents are, well, not very important?

One way to do this is to imagine a magnifying glass. Nothing fancy, just a normal lens on a handle. Then imagine it's a sunny day and the glass is catching some sunlight. It takes that light and concentrates it on a point.

So now the metaphor: that point is you. The magnifying glass is your parents, and the sunlight is the collection of themes that transcend your particular historical parents: love and joy, relationship to fear, social rules and boundaries, fear of death, possibilities in relationships, etc. The gamut, in other words, of all those universal elements that make up the whos and whats of our identity.

So the light—the important elements of human life that describe who we are as individuals—is magnified by the figures of our parents. Each different lens magnifies and colors the light that passes through it in different and particular ways, i.e., us, the child. The light is not synonymous with our parents; it doesn't come *from* them, they just craft it in a certain way. Still, all the rays of light that passed through that lens are still there at the concentrated point—i.e., again, us—just to different degrees, in different intensities.

As applied to psychotherapy, there is a very practical reason to explore your parents and your relationship to them: by understanding them and your relationship to them, you get to see more clearly and intensely your particular *bending* of the universal human qualities represented by the light. It's not an effort in blaming. It's not a project in limiting ones complexity or breadth. It doesn't exclude important other forces. It's simply a good place to read about oneself.

And, of course, the point of that examination is not more navel-gazing; rather, the point is the seeing of one's particularity (the bend of the light) and one's universality (everyone is a collection and magnification of the same rays). The more clearly you see those two, the more accurately you know yourself, the more skillful you make your choices, and that, indeed, is how we get free of suffering.

# ESSAY 21: MINDFULNESS IS NOT ENOUGH

I picked up a book called "The Zen Path through Depression," (1999) by Philip Martin, to read on the plane the last time I headed East (that's a Buddhist joke...). It's a very warm, humanistic take on depression, focusing on the application of Zen Buddhist philosophy and practice to the challenge of overcoming depression. It's well and simply written, and I think its main virtue is the inspiration it might offer to those who are burdened by depression.

But where the book falls short, in my opinion, is in not putting itself within a more integrated model of how one actually tames depression. There is *certainly* nothing wrong with inspirational books; when you're flat on your face, it can be a great relief to know that others have gone through it and survived, that there's possibility and hope.

The difficulty comes when one understands depression (and anxiety) as *systemic* problems, which get more so the longer they have existed. Depression lodges in the body, the heart, relationships, cognition, and relation to Spirit. In my experience, in order to bring it to heel and keep it docile (en route to transforming it permanently), it must be addressed in all those areas with an integrated strategy.

Other disorders or problems can often be healed quickly and directly, if their roots do not go very deep (say, being depressed over the loss of a job, or perhaps a phobia about spiders). But chronic depression does not have a quick fix; it requires you to go after it from different angles, and keep after it. That is why depression offers, ironically, the potential for such deep transformations in a person: in order to make lasting changes, the *person* has to change lastingly. No panaceas.

So my little cautionary note about what is otherwise a laudable work on Mr. Martin's part, is that without setting his book in an integral context (that is, stating that he is just focusing on a part of the puzzle), there is the possibility of implying that what he's describing is *the* path. While mindfulness might be the key to enlightenment, in my view, in overcoming depression it is the cornerstone...but not the whole house. As the scientist might say, it's necessary but not sufficient.

I say this not to criticize Mr. Martin's work, but in order to highlight the fact that spiritual practice casts its own shadow, in the form of ignoring the "grungier" realities of life. In the effort to transcend, seekers often overlook the Spirit all around them. And when such a seeker is struggling with depression, the danger is that, in emphasizing the "transcendence" of the path, they miss paying attention to the needs of the body and the heart. I've sat with folk who have meditated for 20 years and who struggle with shame over not having left depression behind, who have put all their eggs in the basket of their path such that other important factors are overlooked. Like eating well and consciously (speaking of eggs...).

All parts of creation are deserving of their due, which is particularly true when you are trying to overcome depression. Absolutely, meditate and practice faith...then go for a run, call your friend, eat your salad, and get enough vitamin D. All of it needs to be part of your work to deconstruct depression; overly focusing on one aspect of depression, giving it a greater significance that it actually has, leads to a baffling condition where you're "doing it right," and yet the depression isn't moving. The reason for this is succinctly given by H.L. Mencken quipped, "For every complex question, there's a simple answer—and it's wrong."

# ESSAY 22: QUESTIONING AND EXAMINING DEPRESSION

For some time Howard Cohn has offered a public meditation group every Tuesday evening in the Mission district of San Francisco. This last week I had, unusually, an evening off, so I went to sit with him and his students. It's getting into the thick of S.F.'s winter, with a growing number of cold, foggy or overcast days, so Cohn took the opportunity to speak about depression and meditation.

He began by throwing out the provocative assertion that perhaps 90% of individuals are walking around with some level of depression. Not meaning that so many people are disabled by depression, but that so many folks are suffering from extended moments of what might be termed a suppression of aliveness. This muting of the possibilities of connection and awareness often stems from a largely subliminal belief in one's own insufficiency. We feel ourselves to be lacking, and then the world looks either similarly bleak or impossibly better then us. Our physical energy disappears and our willingness to be engaged (who wants to be engaged with *that*?) dribbles away.

So what does one do?

One technique he offered was simply examining the evidence. What proof is there that one is fundamentally *lacking*? Taking the claim of existential failure at face value, how would you argue it in court? Put together a brief for the judge and see if it holds up. Cohn's claim was that it never will, that depression actually sustains itself by tricking you into not looking into its own assertions. And, the act of looking itself is curative, since when you are looking *at* depression, you forget to identify yourself *with* depression.

Then the other practice is that which meditation teaches: look inward at the raw experience of depression, and really see what it is. What are the emotions? The sensations? The thoughts? How do they weave together to create that which we label "depression"? And what happens when we actually investigate it? What you'll inevitably and eventually find is that depression is a tinker toy construction that at its base has no essential substance, any more than the house you build with these toys is really and essentially a house.

This is not to say that depression isn't real or painful, or that meditation is the only real treatment. Cohn made the point that when depression settles into the body, becomes locked in there, then often a person will need other help (medication, body work). But what one comes to realize in turning towards depression and asking it some serious questions, is that it's not what it says it is. That when the curtain is pulled aside and the real nature of the Wizard of Oz is revealed, you can start regaining the energy of yours that has been trapped in depression.

# ESSAY 23: KEN WILBER ON SHADOW

Here is Ken Wilber's remarkably concise summation of the relationship of psychotherapy to Buddhist practice, and of the way in which "shadow" elements of our psyches inhibit growth. ("Shadow" refers to those parts of us which were, for various reasons, cast out of our sense of self, and left behind as the rest of us continued to mature. These parts, as Wilber points out, remain as grown up as they were when we tried to deny them, but despite our attempts to leave them behind, they continue on within us. For instance, if as a child you realized that Mother was threatened by your anger, you are likely to have suppressed it in service of protecting that relationship (which a child feels almost totally dependent on). Later in adult life, you'll find that when anger does arise, it will often have the quality of a young child's anger, for the very reason that it *is* still so young.)

**Question:** So assuming that this consciousness holarchy exists [i.e., developmental stages]—we were talking about the fact that higher stages can be sabotaged by repressions at lower stages—the internal civil wars.

**Wilber:** Yes, I think so. If the self represses or dissociates aspects of itself, it will have less potential left for further evolution and development. And sooner or later, this will drag development to a halt.

I don't mean to quantify this in such a simple way, but as a crude example, say the self at birth has 100 units of potential. And say that in its early growth it dissociates a small blob at moral stage 1 [referring to the psychologist Kohlberg's pre-conventional stage of childhood development]—say it splits off 10 units of itself. It arrives at moral stage 2 [Kohlberg's conventional stage] with 90 units of its potential.

So the self is only 90 percent there, as it were. Ten percent of its awareness is stuck at moral stage 1, stuck in this little unconscious blob residing in the basement and using its 10 percent of awareness in an attempt to get the entire organism to act according to its archaic wishes and impulses and interpretation [e.g., a man's attempt to get completely unconditional love from his wife, when that is a child's wish that simply cannot be fulfilled in adulthood].

And so on, as growth and development continues. The point is that, by the time the self reaches adulthood, it might have lost 50 percent of its potential, as split-off or dissociated little selves, little blobs, little *hidden subjects*, and these little subjects tend to remain at the level of development that they had when they were split off.

So you have these little barbarians running around in the basement, impulsively demanding to be fed, to be catered to, to be the center of the universe, and they get very nasty if they aren't fed. They scream and yell and bite and claw, and since you don't even consciously know they are there, you *interpret* this interior commotion as depression, obsession, anxiety, or any number of neurotic symptoms that are completely baffling.

**Question:** So this would sabotage higher growth as well?

**Wilber:** Yes, the point is that these dissociated selves—these little hidden subjects that are clinging to lower world views—will take up a certain amount of your energy. Not only do they use energy themselves, your defenses against them use energy. And pretty soon, you run out of energy.

And yes, this will very likely sabotage higher or transpersonal development. Let's say it takes 65 units to get to the psychic or subtle levels [Wilber's names for the certain transpersonal stages]. If you only have 60 units left, you're not going to make it. This is why, in broad terms, we want to integrate Freud and Buddha, we want to integrate lower "depth psychology" with "height psychology" [i.e., a psychology that is concerned with the "higher," or spiritual stages of development].

And, in fact, we are at an extremely auspicious moment in human evolution, because, for the first time in history, we have access to both Freud and Buddha. The profound discoveries of the modern West—the whole notion of a psychodynamic unconscious, which is really found no where else—these discoveries can be integrated with the mystical or contemplative traditions, both East and West, for a more "full spectrum" approach.

**Question:** The point of uniting Freud and Buddha is that if you've got 50 units of your consciousness trapped in the basement, you're not going to make it to the higher levels, as a general rule.

**Wilber**: As a general rule. If you don't befriend Freud, it will be harder to get to Buddha.

So what we do with "depth" psychology—well, actually, that's misnamed. It's really shallow psychology, it's really dealing with the lowest and shallowest levels of the holarchy, *but for just that reason,* their narrow and narcissistic perspective can be so *crippling.*

But the point is, with "depth" psychology, we re-contact these lower holons [i.e., a whole that is also a part of a larger whole] and expose them to consciousness, so that they can be released from their fixation and dissociation and rejoin the ongoing march of consciousness evolution. They can get with the program, as it were, and cease this backward, reactionary, anti-evolutionary pull from the basement of your awareness. They can be reintegrated with your main self, so that your central self might now have 70 or 80 units of its potential available to it, and with that energy it can then continue its growth into the transpersonal.

And if that happens, and transpersonal growth is engaged with great intensity, then at some point you will climb not just up the ladder, but off it. As Zen would say, you're at the top of a hundred-foot pole, and yet you must take one more step. How do you step off a hundred-foot pole? You take that step, and where are you?

When you step off the ladder altogether, you are in free fall in Emptiness.

(from *A Brief History of Everything* (1996), p. 154-156)

# ESSAY 24: WHY DISSECT THOUGHTS?

I was recently experimenting with meditating on thoughts per say, and describing to my wife the curious experience of breaking a thought down to its components. She got to hear about how the thought, "I left the cell phone in the car," was constructed from an image of my truck, a felt sense of the time it takes to walk from my office to the parking spot, an image of where the phone was plugged into the recharger, and a trace of anxiety around fetching it before my next appointment. Her response was a curious, and brilliantly direct, "And why would you want to do that?" Here is how I tried to answer her:

1) By working with thoughts as phenomenon, and breaking them down into smaller, linked parts, you develop an experiential understanding of the fundamentally *composed* nature of thought. Which means that your mind comes to see that thoughts are not reality, which is simple to get conceptually—of course a tree in your head isn't a tree you can perch in—but harder to hold onto as experience when life is moving fast and you are under pressure and stress. Slowing down very ordinary thinking, and *experiencing* what your thoughts are made of, allows the mind to remember its own impermanence when in the heat of life. I.e., meditation creates new habits of relating to experience.

2) By taking a particularly stressful thought—e.g., "My life is sinking like a stone"—and stepping out of this thought by way of dissecting it, you can defuse the power of the thought to determine your mood, emotions, or assumptions about what is possible or not. If you take the thought above at face value, as a statement of truth, then you are probably going to feel some mix of depression, despair, fear, anxiety, and maybe panic. Which means that you'll likely drift towards survival mode, where the mind focuses on which actions might guarantee...well...staying alive a bit longer, and the "extraneous" options are set aside. You are unlikely to respond to such a thought-as-reality with, "Hmm, time to build a bird house for the finches." In other words, this

thought would strongly pull for a narrowing of perspective.

But by stopping and observing the thought, by slowing it down, isolating it and projecting it up on the classroom screen in your mind, you get to see its pieces, the fragments that are stapled together to construct that which would otherwise, when seen at a certain speed, look like a coherent and real *thing*. Like a piece of film through a projector, when you pop it off the reel and examine it, you see discrete frames, holes in the side, scratches, taped edits, etc.

And the purpose? It's not to render thought useless, but to remind the mind that thoughts are incredibly creative ways to piece together the data of a life, but creative does not necessarily translate as *accurate*. A very healthy doubt arises about one's own thoughts and thought process, allowing a stepping back, which in turn opens up possible avenues of action which otherwise are lost.

3) At a deeper level, as with all meditation, analysis of thoughts continues to accumulate proof that no thing is whole and final, but, as Buddha taught, all things are constructed, including our selves. The self that we desperately defend, assembled just like a single thought, is shown as that much less substantial, that much less permanent, and at the end of this process, we see that the self is thoroughly impermanent. Meaning there's nothing to defend, and what a relief that is: we can *really* stop struggling to keep whole what it inherently and unproblematically *broken*!

4) In the meantime, though, there's a remarkable sense of freedom and energy that comes from pulling apart a thought in this very controlled way. Perhaps, like smashing an atom, the energy that's used to hold it together is freed up, leaving us to feel that delightful sense of undefined *potential*.

# ESSAY 25: THE BIG MIND PROCESS

Sitting with big souls, those who e e cummings called "Delectable Mountains," is certainly an invaluable, irreplaceable experience...but YouTube is a decent second. It doesn't replicate what happens in the physical presence of great teachers and beings, but it can give you a hit, in addition to getting a different take on people who otherwise would only be known from their writing or from hearsay. (The popular philosopher Ken Wilber is a good example of the benefits of online video: many, many people I've talked with have an image of him as an arrogant narcissist, derived from his books and sometimes just photographs. But seeing him speak on video, you get a much different picture, of someone with a deep compassion and wisdom often couched in a genuinely deep sense of humor and play.) People whom in the past you would have had to travel to various mountain tops to meet, now you can Google-and-click in a few seconds. And as long as we are clear about the difference between video and face-to-face contact, then the YouTubes of the world are extremely valuable. Of course, you can get lost in tracking down backflipping dachshund videos, but all light casts a shadow...

So in this vein, I'd like to point your attention to the work of Genpo Roshi, abbot of the Kanzeon Zen Center (Salt Lake City), who has developed and is teaching what he has named the "Big Mind Process." Big Mind is an extremely clear example of the meeting of Buddhist insight/orientation and psychotherapeutic methods. It seeks to use what's called "subpersonality work," in the form of Hal and Sidra Stone's Voice Dialogue method, to allow you to gain an experiential glimpse of the enlightened ("Big Mind") mind. The novelty of Genpo Roshi's approach is that, unlike the traditional muscular approach to ego that is taught in the Zen tradition, he works *with* the different parts of the psyche, essentially acknowledging them and their value, and then asking them to step aside so that Big Mind might appear. In particular, the part of our mind that is charged with defense, the "Controller," is, like an actor on stage, asked to speak its piece, and then move downstage to allow other parts, particularly the "non-seeking mind" to move upstage. His idea is that, since Big Mind is "always already" present (in Ken Wilber's term), and is characterized by non-striving, non-struggleling, then having the striving parts of the psyche step aside allows their antithesis to be seen.

Whereas Voice Dialogue is about understanding and improving the relationships between our subpersonalities, Big Mind is about working with ego in such a way that it unlocks itself.

For working with depression and anxiety, this is an extremely important point, even if you don't click with Big Mind Process per se. One of the great underpinnings of these moods is our commitment to struggle, to making ourselves "better" and getting rid of what we don't like. It doesn't work, as much as we may try, or at least this struggle doesn't work for long.

So this point about becoming more allowing and intimate with our less desirable parts, even depression and anxiety themselves, is really critical. Cultivating the capacity to not struggle is, ironically, that which allows us to overcome depression and anxiety, and arrive at genuine (not aggressive) control.

I'd encourage you to check out Genpo on YouTube and see what you think.

## ESSAY 26: IDENTIFICATION AND AVERSION

It has been raining heavily in San Francisco these last few days, in counterpoint to what has been a pretty dry winter. Last night, hail the size and shape of ball bearings clattered down for about a minute, covering the streets and cars in pointillist whiteness, and then, gone, followed through the night with stabs of rain, and a clear sky this morning.

S.F. is similar to Boston, where they quip that "If you don't like the weather, wait fifteen minutes." I've always preferred these storms to the long stretches of overcast—"pointless clouds" as a friend recently put it—that characterizes winters in my home town, and it's probably not coincidence that I've ended up in a town with such micro-variable weather. There's a sense of aliveness in the clatter and crash and flash of a decent storm that's hard to find in days of dim light and canvas-simple clouds.

Now, as I sit in my office, there's medium-heavy rain slanting down onto the roofs below the balcony window, and sunlight slanting through my French doors, through some gap in the clouds. I notice that I like it. And that noticing gets me to thinking about what one does in a life with the experience of "liking," and what it means to manage "liking" skillfully or unskillfully.

The "pointless clouds" used to affect me deeply. My mood would often track up or down according to whether the sky was hidden or not, which went largely unnoticed until I was walking down a hill in North India, under one of these pointless skies. Suddenly the bondage of having my mood selected directly by the weather pattern became starkly obvious. "This has to change," I declared to myself, and over the years it substantially has.

Yet all deep patterns have increasingly subtle layers; like strata of rock, all of the same composition, but with the course gravel on top, pebbles under that, sand below, and fine dust at the bottom. As you dig through a pattern or habit of mind, you will go through levels of course and fine expressions of the same pattern. So it is with the preference for types of weather, having cleared much of the gravel, sitting here in my office I notice some of the sand or dust. It can't be denied: I notice the visceral, sensual effects of the light versus the gray clouds, the thoughts of "I like" or "I don't like." Affinity definitely exists.

But the recognition of like and dislike does a funny thing: it exposes the experiences as relative and constructed. And this offers a very important opportunity to change one's proclivities from something one identifies with ("I'm just a person who hates to be in nature") and therefore must rigidly defend ("Stop ASKING me to go hiking! You KNOW I'm not that sort of person!"), to something more akin to raw information ("I notice that when I'm in the woods, I feel an uncomfortable prickly sensation in my back."). Then you are free to act on it in different ways, more fluidly and openly, without ruling out whole swaths of experience ("Oh! I get it. If I get enough rest while hiking, and don't go for long, I can actually enjoy being on the trail!").

Applying this to my overcast aversion: if I decide that I am simply a person who cannot deal with this type of weather (identification), then I might move to a sunnier climate, or stay indoors, shades closed, hunkered down till the sun comes out. Or I can see that the overcast has certain effects on me— sluggishness, dimmed vision, etc.—and decide as occasions arise what to do, rather than just have one reaction to fit all situations. Some time I might sit with the slowness and see what joy is in that. Other times, maybe when I'm at work, I might turn on the lights and have some coffee. Another time, I might ask a friend about their different experience of the weather and experiment with taking that on like an actor. And so on.

The point being that by dis-identifying from likes and dislikes, you don't become a bland person, but actually come to know your "working" self more intimately, the result being greater freedom and flexibility. Or more simply, not being tied down by your own likes/dislikes, you become happier.

# ESSAY 27: COGNITIVE DISTORTIONS

Daniel Goleman has written a follow-up to his book Emotional Intelligence, his 1995 work which argued that there are various *lines* of intelligence, not simply a cognitive, logical thinking. His second book, called Social Intelligence, focuses in on the neurological underpinnings of social relationships, giving a rather startling amount of evidence for the way in which human brains are structured to be social. For instance, he describes "mirror" and "spindle" neurons whose purpose is to create the ability to feel what another person is feeling, *literally* feel, as they duplicate the experience we perceive others having. There are varying degrees of aptitude at empathy—you can probably scan your friends and identify those who seem to always know what others are feelings, and those who struggle to feel into another person's experience—but every human brain is wired for empathy, for literally resonating with others.

However, Goleman makes the point that, in humans, what interpretation is given to a scene will determine how the brain and body react. He writes about an fMRI (Functional Magnetic Resonance Imaging, a way of mapping the brain's activity) study at Columbia University:

> *How sad. That poor woman standing there all alone, in front of that church, sobbing. The funeral must be going on inside. She must miss horribly whomever she's lost...*

> *On second thought, that's not a funeral. There's a white limo decorated with pretty flowers in front of the church—it's a wedding! How sweet...*

Such were the thoughts of a woman as she studied the photo of a woman weeping by a church. Her first glimpse suggested to her the scene of a funeral, and she felt herself fill with sadness, her eyes welling up with tears in sympathy.

But her second thought changed the photo's impact entirely. Seeing the woman as attending a wedding and imagining that happy scene morphed her own sadness into delight.  As we alter our perceptions, we can change our emotions.

....[With such situations as the woman viewing the wedding photo] the first emotional response happens so quickly and spontaneously that as the amygdale [the part of the brain responsible for assessing danger and triggering fight or flight responses] triggers its reactions and activates other brain areas, the cortical centers for thinking have not yet even finishing analyzing the situation...

The intentional reappraisal of the photo (*It's a wedding, not a funeral*) replaces the initial thought with a new one and the first flood of negative feelings are replaced with a happier dose, initiating a cascade of mechanisms that quiet the amygdale and related circuits...The greater the activity in certain prefrontal areas [areas responsible for the slower assessment or analysis of experience], the more muted the amygdale becomes during the reappraisal.

...As Marcus Aurelius said millennia ago, pain "is not due to the thing itself, but to your estimate of it, and this you have the power to revoke at any moment."

Thinking sometimes gets a bad rap in both spiritual and psychotherapy circles.  For instance, in my training, cognitive therapies (those which focus on the identification and conscious modification of thoughts in order to regulate feeling) were seen as shallow and of limited use, compared with "depth" psychotherapies (those focusing on how a person unconsciously makes meanings of their experience).  And in Buddhist circles, thought can be maligned for its problematic qualities, and not given the respect due to something that, in the day-to-day world, exercises so much influence.

Goleman's work is intriguing because it shows how quickly the mind produces mood out of thought, and also how important it is to examine one's thoughts and experience.  It also says that psychotherapy, by changing what we habitually make out of a situation, literally alters the way the brain functions, making new habits and dissolving others at the neurological level.  For all their importance and life-saving potentials, it is not only medications that alter chemistry and mood/emotions.

This means that thinking is *serious*.  Spiritual traditions have long encouraged students to cultivate certain patterns of thought, recognizing that how you think largely influences emotions and behavior, and more deeply, the fact that thought patterns can *change*, and can be changed through practice.  Cognitive therapy has arrived at the same insight, and has various practices to bring the forebrain to the forefront (as it were) in the endeavor to shift a person's suffering.

In chronic depression, for instance, one can identify so-called " depressogenic" thoughts," thoughts that lead to a cascade of negative moods, and to the firing of their understructure of neurological circuits. This can lead to a looping of thought and mood and bodily experience that produces a major depression, which is intensely painful and difficult to get out of. Suicide is not uncommon for those suffering from depression; as I said, thinking *is* serious.

You can try a simple exercise from cognitive therapy to check this yourself:

1) Think about a situation that is causing you grief in your life, and write down a description of what's happening.

2) Write down how you feel about the situation (e.g., scared and resentful). Rate the intensity of each feeling (0-100).

3) Next, write down what your thought is about the situation (e.g., "My boss really has it in for me.").

4) Think about what kind of distortion this might be (e.g., overgeneralization, minimizing—you can search the internet for "cognitive distortions" and find a list of the 10 classic distortions).

5) Write down what a "rational response" (i.e., your forebrain, not your amygdale's, response) to counter the original negative thought. For instance, "I recognize that my boss is under a lot of stress with the new project that was dumped on him, and is taking it out on me because he doesn't know how to deal with the stress." Rate how much you believe it (0-100). If it is very low, then keep trying to find a thought/interpretation that actually feels more believable or true to you.

6) Go back to your original thought and see, now, how much you believe it, and then check in to what has changed in your mood or emotions.

This is a much slowed down version of what can be developed into an incredibly valuable skill, of checking first impressions or habitual beliefs to be able to see and feel the world more accurately. In doing an exercise like this, you can experience directly what Goleman is describing, that if the brain is seen as a watershed, then thought (or interpretation) is what makes the rain course down one side of the mountain or the other. What gives you a rock-throwing waterfall, or a placid mountain lake.

# ESSAY 28: THE DOING AND NON-DOING OF TREATING THE WILD MOODS

The treatment of depression and anxiety comes in two forms: the management of the symptoms in order to avoid overwhelm, which inevitably means more or less skillful manipulation of experience—the "doing" of treatment; and the endeavor to find acceptance and a mere knowing of the experience—the "non-doing" of treatment.

With the "doing", it is vital to develop the ability to track, in detail, the way in which different parts of the mind and body dance their way into depression or anxiety states. For instance, you'll be going along fine, enjoying the sunshine while driving, then stopping at a light behind a few other cars, and, boom!, you get a surge of anxiety. Being able to break down the experience can make you aware that the car ahead has a bumper sticker advertising chickens. You saw the image of the chicken, and had a memory association of your mean uncle's farm. You felt a clenching in your gut that brought up another memory, of being five and having to stay for a week with the uncle, a miserable, disempowered experience. Your uncle will be at Thanksgiving this year, and at that thought you felt like that five year old, having to be around him without being able to stick up for yourself.

Without being able to track in this detailed way, you are likely to end up with the wrong source of anxiety (as you try to pin the feeling somewhere, anywhere), and therefore the unskillful or inappropriate response. But recognizing what was the relations of body-thought-emotion, you both step away from the whole pattern and see it *as* a pattern (often a relief in itself), and are able to then actively reassess the thought process, or beliefs, that got to the anxiety attack. In the above example, you realize, oh, the anxiety is coming out of these associations, and you know what, I'm not actually without power, I can choose to not go, or when there, confront my uncle's behavior if need be. You'll know if you got the source/sequence right, because your body will relax and you'll generally feel like an adult again.

This is a subtler aspect of the "doing" work, when you are not overwhelmed, when the (in this case) anxiety is not intolerable. But when the symptoms do get to the point of overwhelm, then the "doing" work is to use whatever various skills you have to quell the sensations and thoughts in order to do what has to be done. From the example above, you can see that while you might have some space and time to do the analytical tracking, when the light turns green, knowing how to, say, use deep breathing, or affirmations of safety become extremely useful. These strategies make it possible to move through the world of necessity and responsibility...and of large, fast-moving metal objects.

Then at the "non-doing" level of treatment, the work is not in analyzing the experience, but rather it's about opening to and accepting whatever is in the experience. The effort is to merely experience or observe whatever is happening, in the mind or heart or body. The attitude is expressed as: Oh, look, anxiety...with tight stomach, blurred vision, pounding heart, sense of dread. Oh, look at that. Let's see what happens if I just observe and feel.

This is definitely (and a little ironically) a practice, because as you settle into "non-doing" mode, part of you will jump and say, "Are you crazy, you're in danger! Move! Do something!" and then your mind (and brain: neurology counts) is back in survival mode. The work is to remember the "non-doing" (or, if overwhelmed, to use soothing techniques—the affirmations, breathing, etc.) and to come back to that mindset. Practicing the "non-doing" over and over again until it become more of a habit then the habit of believing the anxiety.

Why the "non-doing"? Why not just focus on the "doing," the management, and once that's under wraps, call it a day?

The reason is simple to state: it doesn't work for long. The patterns that generate anxiety and depression can be managed, but ultimately our management strategies will wear out. We can't keep a good volcano down, as it were.

So the "non-doing," the mode of mere observation, or curious exploration without any injunction to change *anything*, what does that do? Well, the efficacy of non-doing is that, by not participating with the mood, by stepping back and out the whirlpool, we stop giving it our energy. And whatever is not fed begins to wither away.

So the important point of this essay is that the "doing" and "non-doing" are just two sides of the same practice: managing anxiety and depression to prevent overwhelm, and observing these emotions to feed the process of them breaking down. Like a coin, the two sides can't be separated, and to be effective in taming these wild moods, both are utterly necessary.

# ESSAY 29: THE 10 "BENDINGS" OF SPIRITUAL PRACTICE

Jack Engler kicks off the recently published anthology, *Buddhism and Psychotherapy Across Cultures*, with a punchy essay entitled "Promises and Perils of the Spiritual Path." In it he makes the assertion that,

> "[W]e cannot help but assimilate our approach to Buddhist practice [this applies to any spiritual practice] into our preexisting emotional patterns, some of which are inevitably maladaptive. Assimilation is inevitable. It unavoidably affects not only our work and relationships but the way we understand, practice, and experience Buddhist teaching."

He later speaks about the unavoidable *multi-determined* nature of behavior: our choice of spiritual path, spiritual practice, spiritual teacher (not to mention psychotherapist) is a confluence or combination of desires and intentions. Pure desire for transcendence comes along with, say, the desire to find a perfect mother figure (when our own real mother failed dramatically). Attachment to a strict teacher can mirror both our intuition about the need for discipline, and our unfinished psychological business with our own very worldly father. "[H]ealthy motives are typically interlaced with one or more other motivations, other meanings practice can have for us, which reflect our fear of change, our fear of freedom, and our grasping at self to allay our anxiety."

So below is Engler's list (quoted from *Buddhism and Psychotherapy Across Cultures*) of the 10 major ways in which spiritual practitioners "bend" their understanding of truth (as in, how light bends in distinct ways when projected through certain lenses). But, as Engler writes, "We need to be aware of them, not as personal faults or failings, but as the irreducible 'impurities' that need to be refined in the fire of practice."

1) *A quest for perfection and invulnerability.* Enlightenment can be imagined as a heaven-sent embodiment of a core Western narcissistic idea: a state of personal perfection from which all our badness, all our faults and defilements, have been expelled, a state in which we will finally become self-sufficient, not needing anyone or anything, above criticism and reproach, and above all, immune to further hurts or disappointments. Practice can be motivated in part by this secret wish to be special, if not superior: enlightenment will finally elicit the acknowledgement and admiration that have been lacking. Because narcissistic issues are so pervasive in character development and across every level functioning, this is usually the most important of the ten issues.

2) *A fear of individuation.* Fears, conflicts, and felt doubts and deficiencies—around assuming responsibility, being assertive and competent, living our own life and making our own choices—can be avoided through a defensive pursuit of an idealized "egolessness" or "selflessness."

3) *Avoidance of responsibility and accountability.* The Buddhist goal of freeing oneself from egocentric needs and desires can rationalize our avoidance of anxiety-producing situations: making decisions, accepting responsibility for them, and taking charge of our life.

4) *Fear of intimacy and closeness.* A stance of "nonattachment" can rationalize fears of closeness and the anxieties associated with intimacy: fear of feeling exposed, vulnerable, humiliated, shamed, hurt, rejected, or abandoned. It can rationalize feeling of estrangement and loneliness. It can absolve us from fears and conflicts over sexuality.

5) *A substitute for grief and mourning.* Significant personal loss often brings people into practice, but practice itself can be used defensively to avoid the personal issues and feelings associated with real loss. Mindfulness can be practiced in a way that either dissociates the important affects of mourning—anger, confusion, withdrawal, sadness—or acknowledges these feelings only from a safe distance. Or these feelings can be neutralized through escape into no-self. The longing for reunion with the loved one can be displaced onto the quest for mystical oneness and union.

6) *Avoidance of feelings.* The labeling of aversive emotions "defilements" or "unwholesome" in Buddhist practice can lead to thinking the goal is not to feel any disturbing emotions, and then feeling guilty if you do. Western practitioners often have a problem with anger and its derivatives.

An earnest and sincere Vajrayana student started therapy with me with the request that I help him get rid of his anger, that is, collude with his attempt to avoid facing it.

7) *Passivity and dependence.* Fear and denial of anger, competitiveness, and self-assertion (often masked by a passive-dependent or passive-aggressive style) can be mistakenly viewed as the practice of egolessness and detachment from personal desire. Passivity can also be used to rationalize the fear of disagreeing or taking an independent stance. Codependency can be mistakenly seen as compassionate service.

8) *Self-punitive guilt.* Desirelessness and nonattachment can become the arena for acting out underlying feelings of unworthiness and guilt, as well as super-ego needs for punishment. "Needs are bad, and I'm bad for having them."

9) *Devaluing of reason and intellect.* The emphasis on immediate, nonverbal experience in meditation, and the axiom that "those who speak do not know, those who know do not speak," can justify the histrionic defense of "having experiences" without reflecting on their meanings. It can also seem to promise resolution of obsessional rumination by saying, "Don't think, and thereby reinforce the defensive avoidance of thinking to block self-understanding." On the contrary, "Do not dislike even the world of senses and ideas," the Hsinhsing ming (Song of Faith) says, and "Indeed, to accept them fully is identical with true enlightenment."

10) *Escape from intrapsychic experience.* By trying to "let go" of all aspects of psychological selfhood, we can justify the suppression or repression of anything that arouses anxiety or insecurity, and anything that may stimulate self-awareness. States of Samadhi that have the power to suppress perceptions, thinking, imagery, and aversive emotions can be used to keep the mind relatively free of unwanted thoughts and feelings, substituting "bliss" instead.

The point of this list, in our discussion of the Wild Moods, is NOT to give ammo to our self critics ("Aha, I knew I was one of those number 5's!"). Rather, the point is to highlight the universality of these tendencies: everyone, every single person, has a bias towards one of these "bendings," and more so, that it cannot be avoided. Depression especially will want to personalize what is identified as *our* faults, but Engler's point is that these faults on the spiritual path are not personal. You're going to have one or the other, as a property not of your broken self, but of being human.

So, it's not YOU! But it's yours to deal with, which is the good news, because these "bendings" can be clarified and healed, which is what any of these spiritual paths are about anyway, wisdom and clarification, leading to a diminishment of suffering. These are not statements of doom—"And thou shalt forever be bent…"—but identifications of the way out: what can be seen can be changed, and that change is arrived at through observing the truth of these "bendings," and the more we know them, the less power they have, just like depression and anxiety.

# ESSAY 30: MINDFULNESS-BASED COGNITIVE THERAPY FOR DEPRESSION

Mindfulness-Based Cognitive Therapy for Depression (MBCT) is a very interesting new-ish modality (formulated in the early 90's) for treating chronic depression in adults. It was created by three researchers and clinicians in the U.K. (Segal, Williams, and Teasdale) who received a grant to develop a treatment to address the high relapse rate among sufferers of depression. According to statistics cited in their book (*Mindfulness-Based Cognitive Therapy for Depression*), patients with no history of depression had a 22% chance of having a major depressive episode in a lifetime; those with a history of at least 3 depressive episodes face a 67% chance of having another. Depression seems to be "etched in" to a person's psyche/nervous system over time with more experiences, and this proneness to relapse is what MBCT was developed to address.

Essentially, MBCT is an application of Jon Kabat-Zinn's Mindfulness-Based Stress Reduction work at the University of Massachusetts on the use of mindfulness practice (one form of meditation) with patients suffering from chronic pain. Kabat-Zinn's work shows that for these people who have had little success with conventional pain management, the internal work of mindfulness practice substantially helped in dealing with pain.

So the authors of MBCT worked with Kabat-Zinn in specifying the MBSR protocol for training chronic sufferers of depression in skills that prevent relapse. Their own research shows in people with 3 or more episodes, MBCT cut the relapse rate in half (over the 60 week follow-up period). Apparently, they hit on something.

MBCT consists of a mix of mindfulness practice, of practicing a mere noticing of sensation (vipassana practice), as well as certain thought-tracking techniques from cognitive therapy. It is taught as an 8 week class that focuses on skill acquisition, rather than on psychotherapy per se. Groups are from 8-12 people, a size that tends to pull away from the tendency for it to become group therapy. It's really about learning and practicing skills.

Is it spiritual? Not explicitly, neither in design or execution. It really is mindfulness applied to *healing* and not *transformation*. Kabat-Zinn's research shows that mindfulness practice does have specific health benefits; it does make for a stronger mind and body. In the context of MBSR or MBCT, it may bring someone into a deeper relationship to Spirit (whatever word you wish to use here), but the context is not intended for that and there is no spiritual context given to encourage that insight.

So it's a curious application of age old wisdom to the healing arts. Buddhist teachers that I've known have poo-pooed such modalities as MBCT, as rather shallow, or even making matters worse by making the ego (the false sense of a separate self) more entrenched. And on the other side, medical researchers are showing that it really does have positive health effects. It's where the two traditions—spiritual and medical/healing—are hashing it out most directly these days.

Perhaps what the "medicalization" of mindfulness practice is showing is the limits and strengths of these different approaches to health. This would be the philosopher Ken Wilber's argument, that in order to experience ultimate reality, you need to be attuned to spiritual dimensions of life—the insubstantiality of ego, the pervasiveness of consciousness, the oneness of essence. But if your goal is more limited, then the results will be more specific and more confined (as with MBCT—the authors make no claim that it will bring one to enlightenment). Or as Wilber has said, "Give unto Freud what is Freud's, and unto Buddha what is Buddha." That strikes me as a very sane way of seeing it.

# ESSAY 31: THE IMPACT OF ENVIRONMENT ON THE WILD MOODS

Running in Golden Gate Park the other day, I followed a circuit that tracks major roads which, though not freeways, still have regular traffic in cars. As I ran, I paid attention to my mood and thoughts, partially to see how to make it ease-ier (more ease), and partially as an ongoing education in my own idiosyncratic experience of the effect of exercise on well being.

At one point towards the end of the run, I had to decide whether to take another road-hugging route, or cut down a little path that was mostly surrounded by trees, with grass either close by or underfoot. I chose path #2, and as I entered that path, immediately I could sense something shift.

Two analogies come to mind: if you have ever visited the chiropractor, and had an adjustment to some area that released tension you didn't even know was there...well, it felt a bit like that. Or: it was akin to what you feel when a storm is coming in, especially in San Francisco, as either a quick shift in temperature or barometric pressure. Except internally.

I'd actually forgotten about this experience until today, when I came across a report issued by a group in the U.K. (called *Mind*), which studied the effects on mood of walks taken in "green" areas (and "green" activities like gardening) vs. exercise at urban areas (a mall). The findings are listed below, but to summarize, they found that a substantial percentage of participants reported decreased depression and increased self-esteem in green activities, while an also substantial percentage described just the opposite after the "non-green" exercise.

It strikes me as pretty intuitive that this should be the case, though the report does not try to definitively answer why. (The studies had a number of factors aside from location—such as being part of a group, who your group-mates were, the controlled boundaries of the group vs. the random people at the mall—which make it difficult to just say that nature is the key factor in alleviating depression.) But it does give a spin to the widely accepted and tested connection between mood and exercise, that apparently not all exercise is created equal.

For those of you suffering from depression or anxiety, it is something to experiment with—literally experiment with. Take a 20 minute walk through your neighborhood, then take a walk of equal intensity and length through a park. And then through a forest. Then by the ocean or a lake. On a mountain. In the desert. Keep notes on the differences, on what seems to brighten your spirits, what gets your serotonin flowing, as it were. Pay attention to how the natural world *actually* affects you.

What I find in working with depression and anxiety is this experimental attitude is so important in breaking out of mental loops, in reconnecting or reestablishing contact with the real world, of here-and-now experience. Depression and anxiety are so much about part of the mind telling entrenched negative stories about oneself and the world, so as a method, experimenting with seeing what the world *is* outside of one's stories (without needing to then *attack* the stories) is key to breaking down their toxic effects.

So, here's the summary of the study's findings:

- 71 percent reported decreased levels of depression after the green walk.
- 22 percent felt their depression increased after walking through an indoor shopping centre and only 45 per cent experienced a decrease in depression.
- 71 per cent said they felt less tense after the green walk.
- 50 per cent said they felt more tense after the shopping center walk.
- 90 per cent said their self-esteem increased after the country walk.
- 44 per cent reported decreased self-esteem after window shopping in the shopping center.
- 88 per cent of people reported improved mood after the green walk.
- 44.5 per cent of people reported feeling in a worse mood after the shopping centre walk, 11 per cent reported no change and 44.5 per cent said their mood improved.
- 71 per cent of people said they felt less fatigued after the green walk and 53 per cent said they felt more vigorous.

The broad point to derive from this study is not really that we should always choose the forested path, but that environment, like it or not, affects mood in subtle or not so subtle ways. Paying attention to that fact, and the cause and effects, can lead to an awareness (like with me on my run) of impact that then opens up options to serve our mood by changing our environment. And that could mean that if we're in a mall, we could move from next to the pretzel stand over closer to the fountain, or could walk out of the mall and head for the park. But without that awareness (and acceptance!) that we're being affected, there's no change possible.

# ESSAY 32: HOW MINDFULNESS CLEARS
# THE DOORS OF PERCEPTION

I think it was just last week, while visiting family, that that perennial wistful complaint arose: "Why does it seem like time speeds up as we get older?" We all shrugged and shook our heads and considered the seeming constants of human life.

But Daniel Siegel, in <u>The Mindful Brain</u>, actually gives an answer through the lens of neurobiology, and in doing so suggests why mindfulness practice is enlivening. He doesn't speak specifically of depression, but it might also be a way of understanding why mindfulness practice helps break up the feeling of "deadness" that so characterizes depressive states.

Siegel cites a 2005 study of the sense of subjective time which concluded that "information density" is the key to understanding the waxing and waning of this feeling of time. Information density is defined as "a certain amount of information being perceived and processed per unit of time," and this density increases when an experience does not meet our expectations.

So what are "expectations"? Expectations are memory-based ideas/images of what an experience is supposed to be like. For instance: "Out in the pasture was a horse." An image will arise that is what your history has trained you, through experience, is a horse. These expectations are called "invariant representations" (IR), and are processed in the cortical memory areas (the neocortex of the brain). This area is arranged in vertically arranged columns, made of six layers. The cortex, the outer layer of the brain, is fed perceptual information (brown, moving like such and such, whinnying sound, arrangement of limbs, etc.) which, triggering the IR, allows us to perceive "horse."

But the cortex also sends information back down the cortical layers, which allows the blending of these two streams, the raw sensual and the memory based IRs.

You don't have to intensely study the sense information of your experiencing of a horse to have your brain fire the recognition, "horse!" You could be wrong, which, if you pay attention, you'll see you are all the time in small ways. The shadowy shape under the trees out near the fence is my uncle's horse...oh, wait, actually, with more attention, I see it's the play of light against some stacked hay. (Now IRs of hay bales come to mind.)

What IRs do, in terms of perception of time, is to require less attention to orient ourselves to the world around (or within). We label and move on. This makes for more efficient information processing, but we lose the visceral quality of experience in the bargain. Siegel writes:

> "As we grow into adulthood, it is very likely that these accumulated layers of perceptual models and conceptual categories constrict subjective time and deaden our feeling of being alive. Without the intentional effort to awaken, life speeds by. We habituate to experience, perceiving through the filter of the past and not orienting ourselves to the novel distinctions of the present."

So even if we get the sensory information right—yup, that's a horse—over time, without intentional efforts to shut off the process of inscribing IRs, we end up with relating to the *model* of a horse, rather than the horse right in front of us. And since these models, by neurological design, have a lesser "information density," we find ourselves living in a greyer world if that's all that we "see."

For instance, a client once achingly described this process, at the beginning of their therapy, like this:

> "I feel like what happens if I make some big change—I'll leave a girlfriend, or move houses or cities, ditch a mentor, whatever—and for a while my life feels fresh and open. Then it's like I'm looking through a window without any glass, so what I see is what's right outside. But as I keep looking, the shapes begin to start abstracting, like the image is crystallizing. That grassy patch becomes just a green pane; the house becomes a few colors and shapes. Finally it's as if I'm looking through a stained glass window at the world, just a broad, two dimensional abstract of what was there, with only vague

movement behind it. It's horrible. And then I go and smash it and can see clearly for a while till it starts again."

This is the way the past, in the form of abstracted information fed back to us from the brain's cortical level, intrudes and dulls the present, utterly unique experience. The fact is that there is a model of a horse which genuinely does correlate with experience; the IR "horse" does point to something in the experiential world. (Otherwise, where would we know to put our saddle?) But it cannot, and is not intended to, tell us about the unique creature that stands in front of us expecting a handful of grass.

Mindfulness practice—the intentional orientation of attention to the raw, un-preprocessed experience of the present moment—is a way (psychotherapy another) to *at least* inhibit the grasping of the mind for IRs, if not actually break down old expectations that no longer serve us. It is a training in expanding subjective time, of increasing the "space" of our world, while depression is the exact opposite, the oppressive dominance of IRs over the raucous world of direct experience.

A child literally has not built up the neurological structures to both support (depending on how young) and encode these IRs, so the world feels fresh and new. And raw, which may account for much of the Wagnerian Opera quality of a child's life. But maturation brings a more complex modeling of the world, and the tendency is to gradually shift from direct relationships to mediated relationships. From the things themselves, to the things as they are represented.

To practice mindfulness seems to be a process of recovering direct experience, as well as knowing *when* one is in the present versus relating primarily to IRs. There's nothing wrong or right with either (you wouldn't want to try to drive a car without being able to have the IR of a stoplight), and hating one over the other is like cutting off the arms because you're so enamored with legs.

But the ability to drop out of what a mindfulness teacher once labeled "the dusty world of the householder," into direct experience is the ability to constantly renew and refresh our worlds. That seems like something to work for.

# ESSAY 33: SAM THE COMPULSIVE CHECKER

One of the reasons why HBO's *John from Cincinnati* and *Deadwood* have so resonated with me is that they really (as the shows' creator, David Milch, has expressed explicitly) focus on the social body, made up of so many people playing their supposedly separate parts. Both shows are populated with strong characters, independent, fiercely individual. And yet, it's not until they begin seeing themselves as parts of something large that they start to find some peace.

"As above, so below." Or for this essay, "As outside, so inside." The same truth about external communities—of real people in real places—applies to our internal communities, the mix of personalities that compose our minds. The psyche mirrors the body; both are made up of discrete parts/organs in relationship. And as with the body, when the parts or personalities of the psyche start squabbling, and pull away from each other (become *dis-integrated*), well, then you get trouble.

Daniel Siegel, the psychiatrist and writer on neurobiology, has described a 200 million year old structure of the brain (or "circuit") which has held the eons-old responsibility of keeping humans alive and safe. Siegel calls this circuit the "checker," and describes it as having three jobs. First, to scan the environment for what seems dangerous. Second, to alert you to that danger (heart races, vigilance). Third, to motivate you to do something to feel safe (leave the dark alley, get your partner to see your side of the argument, run from the lion, etc.). Siegel's acronym for this is SAM (Scan, Alert, Motivate), and calls this part of the mind the "checker."

With many people, not just those with obvious symptoms (for instance, Obsessive-Compulsive Disorder), SAM gets out of hand, like a guard at the castle gate, jumping up and shouting at crickets chirping. In other words, being inappropriately vigilant, unable to distinguish between actual and perceived danger. The result, though, is that the castle denizens (the other parts of you) keep getting started into action without being able to find the danger. The alarm call sounds, and you rush out with your spear and all you hear is the crickets.

Yet the guard (the checker) is calling for you to *do something*, and this is where ritual behavior can come from. You settle on something like checking the stove three times before leaving the house, and then do it religiously. When you get back to the house and it has not burned down, well, that's just proof that checking the stove is how your world stays safe. (You might not have these kinds of OCD symptoms, but if you take an honest look at some of things you do to feel safe, they'll likely have the same kind of ritual quality.)

But this is where the guard becomes the jailer. He keeps insisting on these "checkings" as a condition of feeling always safe. So safety becomes welded to ritual acts that are not actually reality based. Instead of being able to test the guard's claims of danger, you learn to just react, because otherwise, if you tell the guard to shut up, he just gets louder and fiercer. As Siegel says, trying to fight a 200 million old being is a losing battle.

So the way out that Siegel teaches is one of integration and, well, love. You stop telling the old coot up on the gate to shut up, refrain from throwing your boots or tin cans, and climb up with him to have a chat. You say, "You know, I am realizing how grateful I need to be for your efforts. You and your ancestors have kept me and my ancestors safe for 200 million years. Without you, I wouldn't be around right now. You truly have kept me alive."

"You know, though, some of the things I have to do to please you are really making my life difficult. [You can list them here, e.g., having to be depressed to feel safe is real suffering, keeps me from relationships and a career, etc.] I really know that you don't want me to be miserable; you're not out to harm me, at all."

"So, what I'm wondering if we can work together in the service of safety? What if we could be a little less depressed tomorrow morning? And maybe in the afternoon, see what it's like to not have to avoid the cracks in the sidewalk on the way to the mailbox? [Again, whatever is appropriate to you.]"

I have seen the same kind of success that Siegel reports with this approach, because, just like relationships with family and friends, understanding of purpose and willingness to collaborate pulls the pillars out from under all the chronic conflicts. The Checker might be skeptical at first—and that's why you titrate the process, taking it in progressive steps—but as long as you try these changes and it sees that you remain safe, then in his eyes the job is being done and he can relax. Meaning you don't get started out of bed so often. Meaning, rest.

# ESSAY 34: LEARNING TO SAY "NO THANK YOU" TO THE WILD MOODS

Overcoming anxiety and depression has a lot to do with learning how to say "No!" then, "No," and eventually, "No, thank you." (There is much to be said about saying "Yes!" but I'll save that for another essay.)

There is a story about the Buddha:

> An old Brahman (of the priestly class in India) was feeling threatened by Buddha and his teachings, fearing that he would lose his congregation and income. He decided that the only thing to do was to go to Buddha's monastery to split his skull. But knowing that Buddha was skilled at logic, the Brahman decided to not talk at all to Buddha, but just to go and commit his deed.

> So the Brahman went to Buddha and approached him while he was alone in his interview hall. The Brahman came shouting and cursing, and Buddha said, "Old man, come sit, tell me your problem."

> Here the Brahman steeled his will, wanting to not be swayed from his determination by Buddha's talk. He kept coming, cursing, and Buddha again said, calmly, "Come, sit, tell me what is upsetting." The compassion of the Buddha cleared the Brahman's mind for a moment, and he did indeed sit down with the Buddha.

> Then the Buddha said, "Tell me old man, what do you do if someone comes to your home and brings you an unwanted gift?"

> "Well, I would not accept the gift."

> "Yes, and so it is that you have come to my house, and brought this unwanted gift of animosity—well, I refuse it. You get to keep it and take it away, since I do not accept it." At which point the cloud of

ignorance lifted from the Brahman and he saw clearly. "How did you learn such a thing, Sir?" The Buddha smiled: "Sit, observe respiration, observe sensation, observe yourself [i.e., meditate]."

Another way of phrasing Buddha's lesson: learn to say "No" appropriately. The Buddha, because of his level of development, could easily say, "No, thank you," but being able to use some force and even some anger at the beginning stages is also good practice. Keep good company, think good thoughts, do not invite in those influences which bring you down.

The Ayurvedic doctor of a friend said it like this: "Negative people, negative thoughts, let them go. Say 'no' to them. Like my 5 year old son. If there is something he doesn't like, which is not pleasant, he says, 'No!' Be like that."

The path to this simplicity is to learn clearly what actually is toxic to us, and that requires examining ourselves and actually seeing, as if we were scientists studying ourselves, what input connects to what result. You may have ideas about this, but all ideas need to be put to the test if they are to be truly useful.

I remember a friend who, for political reasons, felt it both a right and duty to steal from corporate stores. She was pretty attached to her beliefs and their underlying anger (and hurt). Hot off a meditation trip, and practicing the Buddhist precepts (which includes "Not taking that which is not given"), I tried to argue in favor of not stealing (one of the precepts). No go. Then I asked her what it actually *felt* like to steal, whether she experienced pleasure or pain. She was honest at heart, and genuinely wrestled with the question. When she realized that where she *thought* she was acting in her own interest, she actually was causing herself pain, then she stopped. When we realizing we're petting a hot stove and not a kitten, we automatically yank our hand away.

As the ideas of how life should work, or how you should be, gives way to a clearer understanding of what *actually* causes pleasure, what *actually* causes suffering, then the underpinnings of anxiety and depression start dissolving. You become able to manage these moods (when they do slip in your house) much more accurately, knowing more precisely what actions or inactions will feed the moods or let them dissipate.

But more deeply, your system starts learning that depression and anxiety are built up out of other things (low serotonin, suppressed anger, thoughts of despair, etc.) and therefore are not monolithic. These emotions come and they go, and we either put out a banquet for them when they arrive, or we say "No, thank you," and let them out the back. We don't get tricked by their claims of permanence and power; we realize that we do have power to influence our mood, and that makes a world of difference.

# ESSAY 35: NAMING VS. NARRATING

In this essay, I'm going to address the differences between narration (story telling) and naming (identification). It's a big difference, both in terms of the neurological underpinnings, and more importantly, the outcomes that relate to dampening, or ramping up, anxiety and depression.

**Narration**

One aspect, or function, of the human mind is that it can make up stories about its experience: i.e., narration. As an example of this, think of times when you've seen, say, the street in front of your house, and being anxious at the time, interpreted the scene as harboring threats that couldn't be seen. Another time, same street, you step out after having a great, warm interaction with family, and you see the beautiful sunset over welcoming houses and content neighbors. "World is dangerous" might be the title of the first, and "World is safe" might be the title of the second. Both, however are stories, narratives.

Stories, or narratives, are ways in which the human mind (and brain!) string together information and data that comes in from the various senses (including the mind) and constructs a world from this information. With story one above, inasmuch as you believe it is true (that is, you are not questioning its accuracy, and remembering its nature as a story/interpretation), then the outcome is a given: defend yourself and stay vigilant. With the second, the outcome is: enjoy the experience, open to other people, be heart-full, because you are not at risk.

Narratives are both wonderful—I've loved literature since my earliest days— and problematic. And unavoidable: human minds and brains are wired to create meaning from experience, otherwise life would look like the white noise on an out-of-tune television.

The problem is that, if narratives are not understood to be *constructed,* then instead of them serving you (bringing delight, meaning, community, connectedness) the tendency is that you serve them. When you are in anxiety's clutch, then your options for action are stripped. When the world *is* terrifying and dangerous (the story) then you can only defend yourself (the outcome). Or if you believe that human relationship is described by being either predator or prey, then you're likely to approach people differently than if you believe life is about loving and connection.

No story is *wrong*—in a very basic sense, all stories are wrong, or inaccurate— but some lead in one direction and others, well, in another direction. That is to say, stories proscribe direction. If you step on a certain road, you get both the benefits of its direction and safety, as well as the reality that it limits your options.

OK, before talking about "naming," I'll give a story a friend told me some years ago. She was heading off to a meditation retreat, and decided, for a reason she couldn't describe, to see a movie called *Aliens 4*. The film has some pretty gruesome images, and even more disturbing takes on motherhood, which my friend found both exciting and repulsive. Ok, show's done and she heads to her retreat, and pretty soon into the sitting (it's composed of all day, silent meditation), she has the imagery from the film flashing over and over in her mind. "First," she said, "it was annoyance, not being able to control it, then it dawned on me, *we're telling the wrong stories.*"

What she meant was not that, maybe in some kind of religious sense, that the film's story was immoral or unethical or just bad, but that the *outcome* was undesirable, for her. The values of her life were ones of developing affinity and connection with others, but as the film played on and on in her head, she noticed feeling disconnected and leery of others. I.e., the "wrong story."

## Naming

Now, what about naming, and "naming your demons"? To name is basically to affix a label to an experience, to join symbolic language to the other senses, and it can be done with accurately, or not so accurately. To name the thing I'm typing on a banana...not so accurate as to say it's a keyboard. And to name an emotion that has me crying, "happiness," is not as accurate as to name it, "sadness."

This, according to my favorite writers on neuropsychology, Dan Siegel, is a critical issue, because neurologically what happens in story telling and what happens in naming are different in process and result. He describes how, in brain scan studies that had subjects induce emotional distress (say, by remembering a loss in their life), the right brain would become over stimulated, flooded with emotion. (We can all probably relate to this state.) However, when the upset person could use their left brain function of languaging (applying language to), to name the emotional state, the entire brain system would calm down (become less neurologically flooded). As Siegel puts it, "You have to name it to tame it."

The footnote to this—and it's a big footnote—is that the naming has to be coming from a mindful state of observing. It's the difference between, "Oh, sadness," period. "Oh, anger," period. Rather than, "Oh, sadness...oh, I hate it, it's going to consume me, I have to block it quick!" That is actually a narrative, a story *about* the emotion. And you can see how it functions like a story, leading to a predetermined outcome (essentially, "Run!").

Demons are a little more complex than emotions, but they will settle down in the same way when you find their proper name (not tell a story about). If one of your demons is, say, addiction to cocaine, then developing the capacity to name it accurately and objectively separates you and the demon. Remember how many stories, novels, films, campfire tales deal with possession? Unnamed demons are those that *possess* us: we are their servants, and it's they who are running the show.

## Naming Stories

However, to stand apart and name it, "Ah, craving to use, period," and resisting the story that the demon then offers ("You can't survive without me! We are friends! You can't do your career without my help!" etc.) causes the demon to lose power and calm down. (In my head, I'm seeing unmasking of the Wizard in the *Wizard of Oz*.) Practice this over time, and what you're actually doing is depriving the demon (the attachment, the neurological habit, the psychological pattern) of its food, since the demon needs you to buy into its story (to identify with it) to survive. And this dissolution effect is the real power of naming, and why both psychotherapy and mindfulness practice can have such profound effects, can actually transform old demons and merely keep them at bay.

Another way of looking at this process is that demons are toxic stories that very directly control behavior (as in addiction). But any story can also become the focus of naming, of observing and identifying. One does not have to try to rip out stories you don't like; that sort of aggression just lodges the story in further (demons love to fight). Rather, the recognition of a story *as* a story is actually to see things clearly: yes, this is a story. Then you get to decide whether to keep the story or not, indulge in it when it arises, or not.

In other words, *choices* arise out of *naming*. Choices don't arise from (unrecognized) story telling.

**Experiment**

As always, I encourage you to chew on these ideas and see where or how or if they fit for you. Not so much as ideas, but as experiments. Pose some research questions for yourself (e.g., how does narrating feel different than naming, in terms of bodily sensation) and then explore these feelings. Deep change will only come when a deep part of your mind—the part that *experiences* the world, not just thinks about it—understands something new. Until then, it's pretty much an act of telling yourself a rippin' good story.

# ESSAY 36: YOU HAVE TO NAME IT
# TO TAME IT

Following on the "Naming vs. Narrating" essay, below is Dan Siegel (the writer on neuropsychology) on the subject of how "mindful naming" might be working at the neurological level. This extended quote is taken from a teleconference he offered, based on his book The Mindful Brain. It's a bit technical, but has some very interesting things to say about how the calming function of naming might actually work. But perhaps the main point is to further make the point that the brain and neurological system has a structure, and has requirements for its care (as it were). Heroic "choosing" does not work because it's not congruent with the neurological reality, one of which suggested below is that language is required, *neurologically*, to elicit calm. See what you think.

> If those [right hemisphere, emotional processes] are really revved up and don't have the involvement of left hemisphere linear, logical, linguistic understanding then what you experience is understood as an imbalance in bi-lateral integration. Let me be very specific about this....There's a discussion in the *Mindful Brain* about the importance of the mindfulness awareness facet of labeling and describing with words, and there are studies which are reviewed there which suggest that when a person is shown an image of a very emotionally expressive state, their right sub-cortical structures, especially in the limbic area—the fusiform gyrus, which has a face recognition zone, and especially the amygdale—respond in a big way to the affective expression seen on this image in the right hemisphere.
>
> When you ask someone, especially someone for whom mindfulness traits that are high, to label and describe the affective state they see— when they name accurately the affective state they see, it's the left hemisphere naming process, with words, the right hemisphere sub-cortical structures calm down.

Linking left and right in a mindful state of labeling one's internal world, that mindfulness trait, in people with mindfulness traits primarily, it calms the whole system down.

...Here's the proposal: In neuroscience, the left and right hemispheres have what's termed a homologous relationship to each other. There are regions in the right hemisphere that are called homologous with similar but mirror—that is, they are across the corpus collusum on the other side of the brain—homologous regions on the left. These homologous zones on the right and left have inhibitory connections. So in other words, when the left area A becomes active, it calms down the right area A, not the right area B. The left area B would calm down the right area B. So when A right and A left are homologous then the activation of A left calms down A right.

Now here's the hypothesis. The mirror neuron areas—the mirror neurons are these neurons that allow us to embed the state of another person in something we could call resonance or emotional attunement. When the right hemisphere resonance areas become active, including the mirror neurons, and this would included the amygdale—the fusiform gyrus has ways of registering the affective state of someone else—then those areas (and this is the proposal) have a homologous left area which are the mirror neuron language areas. So when we label with words what we are experiencing, you could say, "You have to name it to tame it." That linguistically labeling brings equanimity to the right hemisphere. In someone with a preoccupied state, what we can suggest is that this impairment of the logical left hemisphere to access right hemisphere stuff has blocked the ability of linking the homologous area of the left to calm down the right. That's the overarching proposal. Here we would see, of course, that when integration is achieved, that is, when you have these differentiated areas, right and left, be brought into a functional linkage—the definition of integration—we move from either chaos or rigidity to a state of coherence.

# SECTION 3: EXPERIMENTS

## ESSAY 37: SAFETY AND SUPPORT

Ok, here's a thought experiment. Imagine you've gotten a new motorcycle, and you're going to learn to ride it. A trusted friend who has experience with two wheels takes you to a empty dirt road and tells you the technical details— there's the clutch, there's the brake, gas, etc. Then he has you sit on the bike and start it up, see how that feels. When you tell him OK, he tells you to experiment with first gear as he trots alongside. Then you practice turns. Then...

How does that feel (assuming you've never ridden a bike before—if so, then substitute something else that could be perilous, maybe hang gliding)? Try to really climb onto that bike with your friend and see what that's like.

Now, at the other extreme: imagine you, still a newbie, get this same motorcycle, and the only place to learn is at the edge of a cliff dropping down to the ocean. It's windy and raining, there's mud and sand and you haven't got a helmet. And no one is willing to be there to help guide you. So you climb on and turn the ignition key...

Now, how does that feel in comparison? Really, climb onto *that* bike and see what you feel.

This is the difference between change (in this case, learning a new skill) *with* support and negligible consequence for failure, versus change *without* support and with possible disaster as the cost of not getting it right the first time. And if you put yourself into those two different scenarios, then you have a feeling for the difference in sense of comfort and safety, and willingness to engage the challenge.

But notice that with the first example, there is *appropriate* support. You still have to get on and ride, accepting the inherent risk and facing your fears. It would be much different if your friend kept you in first gear when you were ready for second. Or startled every time you had a little wobble. Or put bubble wrap all along your path. Support and safety have to be geared to what you are doing, and not be overdone.

A colleague who is a Feldenkrais practitioner (a form of bodywork) tells me that in her work, learning happens most quickly when people feel safe, and recognize the pleasure in the new activity. Which kind of flies in the face of the old adage, "No pain, no gain." In fact, she says, the brain is hungry to learn, and as she's seen in young children with severe developmental problems, it can learn new patterns very quickly when it gets that the new way actually feels and works better than the old.

The same is true in psychotherapy: when you really get that the new feels better than the old, you'll swap them out pretty quickly. But that process of change requires the right proportion of support and safety, enough to allow you to be willing to risk the new (there's good reasons why we hold onto old habits) without facing catastrophe for falling on your face. And without having taken away your essential responsibility for being the agent of your own change.

So with anxiety and depression, because of what people have experienced in the severity of the fall (when one has relapsed into a major depression or anxious state), defenses tend to harden. One holds onto what has worked, or kinda worked, pretty hard, because letting go to try something new is pretty scary.

That's why anything and everything that can be done to make it safer to experiment, well, should be done! I remember a friend's account of being on a meditation course, and having gone to the teacher for an interview. "You know, this is a tough sitting, but I don't want to go easy on myself, you know, wander around and look at the flowers. So, my question is, what supports should I accept." The teacher looked at her intently, and after a pause, said, "Well, all of them."

A support by definition encourages your learning. If it's not doing that, then it's either a crutch or a barrier.

Often, with anxiety and depression, having felt the pain of seriously wild moods, we push ourselves too hard and fast and equate "safety" with "stagnation," or we just don't really get the concept. The upside is that much of the time we can manage to avoid the demons, or keep them from catching up to us. The downside is that we can't learn how to effectively wrestle or cajole the demons back into their cages (which would then allow us to actually find out what they are).

So my encouragement to all my clients is to take all the supports they can, and learn to accentuate the places where they do feel safe already, and not to dwell in the places where they feel endangered. What is given attention really does grow, neurologically, emotionally, psychologically, spiritually. And while there is plenty of danger, if a deeper sense of safety can be cultivated (it really can, with practice and support), then one can maintain poise with the demons, which itself turns them into kind of manic puppies.

As an experiment, then, in this moment, see in what way you do already feel a sense of safety. It doesn't have to meet your mind's criteria—"we're safe only when..."—it just has to *feel* safe. If it's nothing in the environment (you're out in a noisy cafe and not at home in your comfy chair), then look through your near or far history for a place or person that felt safe to you. When you find something (how strong or weak the sense is is not that important), then explore that place or person, letting yourself *feel* into the sense of safety they allow you to tap into. Really re-familiarize yourself with that as much as you can. This is the process of cultivating a support, in this case, internal. You can learn to dip into this from time to time when you start feeling unsafe, and can practice being with the sensation of safety and letting this feeling grow as an experience.

Again, it does not have to meet the mind's criteria, which are probably legion for you. Safety, in its essence, is a state/feeling, and being able to access it as such gives you a much greater range of possibility, simply because fear closes the world, and safety opens it.

## ESSAY 38:  THE MAGIC WELL EXERCISE

Have you noticed asking questions of yourself, like, "Am I good enough," or, "Is this all useless," and then wondering why the answers are so elusive?

A colleague who traveled in Asia for a while once told me this story:

> I was in Thailand, in the North where there were a lot of fogged-in days, at least up in the mountains.  My mood was really getting affected after a while.  I was bummed out much of the day, and noticed myself walking around the forest thinking, 'Why can't I shake this?' The question repeated over and over, and I'd struggle with it like a Zen koan, and yet just feel worse for the effort, and thought that I was simply too stupid to figure out the answer.
>
> Then one day, walking back from a dismal hike, coming through the gate of the village I was living in, I asked the question again, but for some reason it seemed to actually come out as a question.  The difference was like, 'Hmm, I wonder what's keeping this in place?' Which may sound similar, but there was a part of me that came online, a rational, data-driven place that, when it showed up, kind of shone a light behind what had been going on.  That what I'd been actually saying was, 'I'm miserable,' but I was putting that feeling in the cloak of a question.  When the cloak dropped off, the answers came quickly and without a lot of struggle.  Like, 'Oh, duh, it's been foggy and I always get low when there's not enough sunlight.  And I'm eating poorly and am far from home.  Oh!' And then the solutions came quickly and with a clarity that allowed me to actually take action.  But it required differentiating between what was a question, and what was me saying, 'Ow!'"

Ironically, too, when I got clearer about me stating a *feeling*, I felt more compassionate towards myself.

So, what is this all about?

Basically, perseveration and rumination are two of the forces that drive and support anxiety and depression. Like my colleague's quandary, they often take the form of asking questions that aren't really questions at all. These are sentences that do, indeed, seem to end with a question mark, and yet are not actually taken up as real questions: they don't actually go through a process towards either being answered, or being tossed out as illegitimate questions. That's how real questioning happens.

My colleague's problem was that he was stating a feeling as a question, but didn't initially realize the difference. So until his rational mind popped up to actually entertain the question ("Why this suffering?") *as* a question, he was just beating himself up for not solving a problem that couldn't be solved in its own terms. When the issue is "I hurt," the answer is not logical but empathic: "I'm so sorry you're hurting." (Try to rationalize with a three year old who has lost a cherished toy about why they are feeling sad, and you'll understand this point.)

In other words, these are questions without rational answers, because they are not actual questions, not actually inquiries. And this is the dilemma, that when we forget what we're actually doing is not questioning (stating a feeling and desire vs. practicing inquiry), then when we don't come up with an answer, we take that as a sign of danger, often thinking, "If I don't figure this out, I'll feel miserable forever." Then, naturally, we try "asking" again, to solve the "problem" of not knowing the "solution," basically trying to find a way to feel safety and control. But with no solid answer coming, we zip around the track yet again. And depending on the question, our "failure" to find "the answer" is going to be either depressing or stokes anxiety.

There are a few ways out of this loop, and I'll offer an exercise below for one way, emphasizing acceptance and openness. I'm calling it the Magic Well, as it's a visualization involving...can you guess? Here goes:

> Closing your eyes, imagine you are in a safe, protected field of grass. It's sunny, mild, a pretty nice place to be. (Change the place if you need to, so long as the sense in your body—the felt-sense— is one of comfort and safety/peacefulness.)

> Now, you see an old fashion well there a little bit in front of you. It has stones around the edge (you won't fall in). This is a magic well, but you have to read the plaque on the side to understand what kind of magic.

> So, what you need to do is think of a question you want answered,

and imagine it as having form, and resting in your upturned palms. Whatever feels like its natural form, pretty or not so pretty, it's all fine.

Now, with your question formed, you walk up to the well and read the plaque: "This is a magic well, magic because it will answer your question. However, it answers on its own schedule. Your job is to ask, and then step back with an open patience. The well's job is to answer."

The well is deep, and you step forward and tip the question gently off your hands to drop down into the darkness. Now you step back and practice the patience of waiting, knowing that eventually, and appropriately, the answer will return to you.

Good work!

For some people, this exercise feels like a relief; for others, letting go of the question, giving it over to the universe, or a deeper part of ourselves (however one thinks about where it goes) causes anxiety. Any reaction is fine. This is an exercise in asking a question differently, and implicitly in developing trust that the answer is known already, in oneself, in the ether, in the mind of Spirit, in your genetic code, and that openness will provide the information better than an insistent demand.

Notice that, in the example of my colleague, his shift in questioning led to a more active problem solving stance. But it started with an openness of questioning, a real curiosity or wondering. He had to be open and accepting, or at least tolerant, of *not knowing* in order to ask the question. The Magic Well is asking with a big openness, allowing something larger to do the answering.

So experiment with what approach seems to work with which question (radical openness, problem solving, mere empathy, etc.), but keep in mind that the starting point is opening to uncertainty and unknown, in order to get a real answer, and that you don't initially know what it will be, but trusting (more and more!) that it will be OK.

# ESSAY 39:  FROM VISION TO ACTION

One of the defining experiences of anxiety and depression is overwhelm, that state where your ability to cope with life collapses.  (Or, as defined by the neurologists, that state where the demands of experience exceeds your "range of tolerance.")  At best, it makes you tired and at worst, it can mean that looking at the dishes in the sink triggers a cascade of fear or exhaustion that throws you onto your most basic of coping skills, usually either fleeing or collapsing.

Now, tackling anxiety and depression requires a multi-pronged approach, from developing spiritual connections, to basic skill building (macro to micro), and with the topic of goal setting, we're on the latter part of this spectrum.  (Although, it's not a black or white issue:  hope can facilitate real-world planning, and having a clear plan can engender hope.)

So here I'm going to take the "clarifying the process" approach, and present some thoughts about goal setting and execution which might be helpful.  I'm trying here to make the steps distinct, because we can get into trouble when we think goal setting is just one process with one method or one step.  Kind of like thinking that any work on a car, simply because it's a car, uses the same tool.  Try fixing the electrical system with a wrench...

**First step:  Vision**

Here's where you are letting your heart and mind fly with desire.  Really.  This is not the time, at the beginning of the goal setting process, to focus on the "hows" of the process.  Vision is about identifying where it is you really, in your heart of hearts, want to go, and getting into the nuts and bolts will very easily chase the vision away.

For instance, it's common to struggle with the question, "What am I going to do with my life?"  We often, at different phases of our lives, seem to run out of a path and kind of stand in an open field looking for direction.  To grab at a goal, the next step, is actually to overlook the necessary stage of figuring out your vision and desire. You could say, "My goal is to make a million dollars in the next year," which is a fine goal, but if you haven't tied it to a vision, down the road you may find that it's not at all what you want your life to look like.

"Envisioning" is where you take some time to sit down in the field and mull over possibilities, quieting yourself so you can check these options against what your heart wants. You treat the "What am I going to do with my life?" as a real, objective question, not as a way of stating despair. (If you're feeling despair, it's much better to just acknowledge it *as* despair and sit with that. Trying to ask a question which is actually a feeling, that's just confusing.)

From asking a question in this way, it rouses your mind to actually engage the question. "Oh, my vision of my life is living in the country, married, with animals and owning a bookstore." That's what might pop out of a vision meditation. Whatever feels true and right to you will be a credible vision— i.e., don't second guess yourself too much.

Also, notice that this statement of vision doesn't say anything about how or where or how long. It's a desire, but it will orient the steps down the line. And what it requires to clarify is actually openness and dreaminess, drawing on the right side of the brain, as it were, to give the left side (linear, logical) some direction and purpose.

(A coda with vision: sometimes your focus is much more narrow, in which case vision tends to be less global. For instance, with the dishes in the sink, although the goal is to clean the dishes, there is actually a vision. It might be to live in a house that is clean and inviting, and then keeping up with the dishes is actually a goal *of* that vision. But to get them done, it's often not necessary to spend a lot of time with this vision phase, though acknowledging the underlying desire can be helpful in motivation.)

## Step 2: Goals

So having articulated your vision, you then have to establish some goals, or the vision is going to remain in the dreamy parts of your brain. Here's where our amazing human inheritance of cognitive reasoning and problem solving comes in. Let's hear it for the pre-frontal cortex!

For the vision above (the house in the country), what could be the goals? Since there are "multiple areas of satisfaction" (house, marriage, bookstore, animals), there need to be multiple goals. And the process of arriving at these goals is the thinking about what you want in terms of the vision. So, with marriage, it might be, "To find a suitable partner within the next year, who is interested in marriage." In a way, it's a mini vision, but more concrete: in the next *year* you'll find a partner, not in some nebulous future.

But you also have to assess the reasonableness of the goal, to some degree. If your goal is, "I'll find a husband/wife within a week," that's not likely to happen. You're stating what you want, within likely parameters. This is the assessment part of coming up with goals: is it doable, all things considered?

In the same way, you'd come up with goals for: moving to the country, buying a house, founding/buying a bookstore. The questions are, "What is the framework of action to realize my vision?"

## Step 3: Planning

Here the left brain is getting even more play, because it's here where you look at the goals and create definable, time-limited steps to realize that goal. And these plans need to be carefully assessed for real-world applicability, that the plan actually is likely to realize the goal, that there is enough energy (in whatever form) for the goal. Etc.

So, for the goal of marriage within a year, the question is: "What do I have to do to actually find a partner within a year?" If the plan becomes, "One date each month," that's both too vague—where are you meeting people and how—and not reasonable in terms of meeting the goal. A more likely plan is, "Sign up for several online dating services, put the word out to friends, and go on at least one date a week." These are definable steps, a timeline, and a way to measure progress (dates/week).

Usually, at the planning stage, you notice there are steps, which even above you can see: you have to join the dating service, and get word out to friends, before you can actually start dating. Once that first step is done, then you actually go on the dates at least weekly.

Which brings us to the final step:

## Step 4: Execution

This is where the rubber meets the road. You've got the broad map, you've got the specific targets, you know which car and how long the trip is likely to take, and now it's time to go!

For the marriage plan, this means actually signing up for the service, and contacting friends. And it's a different set of dynamics at work in doing than in planning. The plan is not the action, as the map is not the territory. Whereas you may have a beautiful, clear, and true plan, if it's not executed, then it's just a pretty map.

So at this step, the issues of motivation and energy come really to the fore. Often, you will get a surge of these through the process of planning, because seeing something as organized and doable is a boost to your confidence and faith. But you may still run into typical fears or hesitations, and this is where you organize the supports to help you move into action.

If you're worried about your desirability as a mate, you might take up psychotherapy to help with the fear, or you may say that for every date you muster the courage to go on, you get to treat yourself to, well, something motivating for you.

The execution stage is about actually putting the plan in action, which may be clear after the other stages, or may require work on "execution" issues (there's a little mini-goal setting exercise here, too), but once the vision, goals, and plan is set in place, it's often *much* easier to move forward, because, hey, you know where you're going and you actually want to go there!

**To sum up**

It is important to see goal setting as a chain of linked, but distinct, stages. If it seems, and feels, like just one mass of activity, then, especially if you're prone to anxiety or depression, the process is likely to lead to overwhelm.

Each stage requires a different approach, and even a different part of your brain coming online. The dream fuels the car, but unless there is an engine and tubes to carry the dream to that engine, it's never going to have any traction in the real world. So, to confuse any one stage for another is to risk never getting that car built and moving.

Good luck with your car building, whether it's a little Matchbox or a deluxe sportster, so long as it's truly what your heart desires.

# ESSAY 40:  SHUTTER WIDE OPEN

Roger sat on the couch and looked extremely uncomfortable at my suggestion that he fully feel the anxiety that was coming up, related to a work situation. Instead of talking *about* the situation, I was asking him to focus on the experience of anxiety itself, in his body.  "I don't really want to do that," he said, looking a bit sheepish.  "Good, so we're touching on a belief about actually *feeling*.  And we don't need to push anything here." He noticeably relaxed at hearing this.  "What is the belief about what would happen if you fully felt the anxiety?" He paused for just a beat, then said, "It would be like backing up to my house a cement truck full of toxic sludge, and pouring it all in through a window." "If you open it up, then you're stuck with the sludge forever." "Yes, forever toxic."

Imagine, though, if Roger really believed, without a doubt, that it would not only help him to get that truck cleared out (it's leaking sludge on the lawn continually, say), but that if he had to let the sludge into his house, the process would inevitably lead to the sludge being washed away totally, and his house would be even cleaner and more comfortable than before (no more fumes wafting in the windows).  If he clearly knew this, wouldn't he dive in to the process of emptying the truck?

So the problem with our stuckness very often is not the feelings per se that we're afraid of, but the intensity of the feelings against our belief that we cannot (or should not) let these feelings pass through.  If we knew ourselves to be a Teflon coated pipe, then we wouldn't care particularly what flowed through us, because it wouldn't get stuck and it wouldn't be mistaken for who we are.

We need experiences of "throughput" in order to brave our own scary places, and it is these experiences over time which build the belief in our ability to not only survive, but thrive from encountering these places.

Adyashanti, one of my favorite wise folk, gives a simple but powerful exercise in one of his talks.  He was addressing a man, a physician, who quit his work because he found that he was very open to his patients' suffering, but unable to let that suffering go once he experienced it. In other words, their pain was becoming his (even physical) pain, without clearing out.

What Adyashanti suggested was an imaginal and energetic exercise. First, you feel the front of your chest, where your heart is, and imagine it opened fully, receptive to who and what is around you. At the same time, you imagine the same is true for the area of your upper back directly opposite from your heart. It's as if the shutters are full open, but anything that comes in is going to be felt and then fly out the back. Regardless of what visits, it will leave out the back soon enough.

If you give it a shot, you'll probably see pretty quickly how relatively unfamiliar it feels to have the back shutters open, even if the front shutters are often not even there (that was the doctor's dilemma). And you'll also notice, once you experience feeling things acutely, *and* then experience these feelings passing through, that your willingness and trust in feeling your experience fully grows, because the belief about being "toxified" is chipped away.

You'll also notice when it's particularly appropriate to shut the shutters, like around people who are particular toxic and you are getting too upset by exposure to them to keep the shutters open. This is a practice in making more subtle your openness, and of building trust that you can survive full feeling, whether of your experience inwardly, or of the outward world.

# ESSAY 41: THE ABCDE'S OF ARGUING
# WITH ONESELF

Martin Seligman's <u>Authentic Happiness</u> is an overview of the so called Positive Psychology perspective. Positive Psychology grew up out of Seligman's reaction to the pervasive focus of research psychology on pathology, on what is wrong and why. His response was to want to do investigate what was *right* and why.

One of the basic contentions of Positive Psychology is that positive traits—love, respect, compassion, gratitude—are real phenomenon that can be scientifically understood and, more importantly, cultivated with practice. By looking at the data, the Positive Psychology folk have demonstrated that while character determines a portion of one's depressive or optimistic bent, there is a big range of traits that can be actively and consciously developed. We are not doomed to our genes.

So here, I want to draw from one of the book's exercises, on the practice of disputing one's own negative beliefs or stories. What follows is called the "ABCDE" model, where:

A: Adversity, what the "problem" is in your view.
B: Beliefs, what stories get automatically told about the adversity.
C: Consequences, what are the usual ramifications of the beliefs.
D: Disputation, the active process of arguing with your own beliefs.
E: Energization, the experience that follows the successful disputation of the negative beliefs.

Since depression and anxiety are fed and maintained by persistent, entrenched negative beliefs, this practice is a necessary one in releasing the grip of these moods. It's not the only way of dealing with such thoughts—body practices and mindfulness of the "emptiness" of thought are other practices to be cultivated. But this arguing is a good one, and the ABCDE gives a shorthand for how to do it. I'll go ahead and quote an example from Seligman, using the ABCDE format:

*Adversity*: My boss told me that he was pleased with some new ideas I presented. He asked me to join him at a big meeting and pitch the ideas to our executive team.

*Beliefs*: Oh, no, I can't believe he wants me to go to that meeting. I'm going to make a fool of myself. I just got lucky in my meeting with him. Those really weren't my ideas, anyway; its stuff a lot of us had been talking about. I talked a good game, but I don't have the depth of understanding I'll need to answer question from the big guns. I'm going to be humiliated.

*Consequences*: I feel intense dread. I can't concentrate. I should have spent my time planning the pitch, but I kept losing my train of thought and ended up doing busy work.

*Disputation*: Hang on a second. This is a good thing, not a bad thing. It's true that I developed the pitch with others, but it's not realistic to say they weren't my ideas. In fact, in our last meeting, I was the one that really got us through the impasse and hit upon the new approach. Almost anyone would be nervous presenting in front of the top executives, but I can't psyche myself out. I'm not out of my depth. I've been thinking about this stuff for a long time. I even wrote up my ideas and circulated it around the department. The reason Hank picked me is because he knows I'll do a good job. He's not going to risk his reputation by putting just anybody in front of his bosses. He has confidence in me, and so should I.

*Energization*: I'm becoming a lot more focused and calm. I decided to recruit a couple of my colleagues and practice my presentation on them. I've actually started to look forward to the challenge, and the more I worked, the more confident I became. I even hit upon a few new ways of saying things that made the whole talk a lot more coherent.

What makes this work effective is honesty; to do the ABCDE you have to be committed to a fair argument. When you win the argument against the voice of doom and gloom, in an above-the-belt way (as above), then that voice will relent. That voice is the part of you that's charged with a very simple sense of safety, and if it deems something is going to be unsafe (you're not ready for the meeting, you're unprepared, you're not strong enough), then it will attempt to sabotage in the service of safety. The voice is ruthless but not actually mean-spirited.

But if you can make a convincing case that, no, actually we are safe, that part of you will calm down because its core mission is to ensure safety. Thus, you are not in a death battle (that only convinces your "safety monitor" that things are indeed not safe), just a friendly argument. But tough, too. Don't give up on what you find is true: pause, breath, and look at the data.

# ESSAY 42: THE CULTIVATION OF AWE

I've gotten to thinking about the experience of awe, especially in how it figures into the project of dismantling depression and anxiety. So the question for this essay boils down to: how does awe affect mood?

Ok. If we start with a brief definition from <u>Websters</u>, we get:

> "Awe: an emotion variously combining dread, veneration, and wonder that is inspired by authority or by the sacred or sublime."

I like this definition because it's pithy, as well as expressive of the "layers" of awe that make up this complex emotion.

**Three layers of Awe**

Dread: this is where the individual ego perceives its smallness in the face of both what is vast, as well as what is impersonal. The small, personal self looks at that which transcends and includes it with dread. It fears its own destruction by mistaking its larger self—that which is sacred or sublime—as something foreign. Imagine your liver chugging along, doing its liver thing, and then suddenly it becomes aware not just of the other organs around it, but of how they connect to it, and how it connects to them. "I'm not just me! When did I get plugged into all this?!" That is, dread.

But then there is the experience of veneration (and perhaps the definition above can be seen as laying out both layers and stages of response to the sacred). The vastness is felt as still separate, but as something that one can have a relationship with (that doesn't lead to one's destruction). Your connection is one of association; you participate in the vastness by bowing down.

Then there is wonder. Wonder does not have the element of fear that is in dread, and often woven into veneration. Here is amazement, and in this expression of awe, there is a forgetting of the small ego self. The participation is one of affinity; you see that you are like the vastness. The experience is openness without fear.

## Awe and Mood

What, then, does awe have to offer people suffering anxiety and depression? In terms of just the management of these conditions, awe is not actually that important. But in my experience, to fundamentally transform anxiety and depression, awe is actually essential. Why?

If depression boils down to alienation—at the mental, emotional, physical, and neurological levels—then awe is its antithesis. Awe is the experience that depends on a recognition of something larger than oneself (re-cognition, a thought about); an emotional openness or resonance that has the three flavors (dread, veneration, wonder); a physical resonance with the vastness, whether echoing fear or joy; and the neurological resonance that actually allows the thoughts, emotions, and sensations to be felt.

It might be too much to say that depression and awe cannot go together; it seems more of a spectrum, where depression increases as awe decreases. I.e., depression holds more dread than wonder, as it is more intense, and awe holds more wonder as *it* is more intense.

So if there was a way to consciously cultivate awe, it would mean in effect consciously cultivating un-depression and un-anxiety. The more of the one, the less of the other. Try having the same door open and closed at the same time. It can't be done. And if it's more open, then it's less closed.

## An Exercise:  Awe location

This exercise in the *location* of awe can be done anywhere, but you need to have time to not be distracted or pulled away to a task. Set aside a fixed amount of time, say, 5 minutes to start.

1) So, imagine you're in a duck blind, out in the grassland, just scanning for the right bird. You're not pressured because that does no good in this situation. The mindset is a meditative one, not an active-doing one.

2) Focusing (for now) just on the visual field/sense, let your visual attention roam over the environment.

3) Notice the objects (the tree, the person, that building, it doesn't matter what it is) and feel their quality. The more depressed you are, the

deader/flatter the object is likely to feel. The more anxious, the more fear-inspiring.

4) Keep scanning till you notice an object which doesn't feel either flat or fearful, that has a quality of openness and pleasure. It doesn't matter *at all* what it is, or what you're *supposed to* feel about it. All that matters here is what that visual object happens to do in the moment as rods and cones are stimulated in the eye, the optical nerve vibrates, that vibration zips into the brain. Etc.

5) Keep your attention on that object and let yourself feel, take in, and open to (as much as possible) the feeling of openness. See if the feeling approaches awe in some form or intensity. Even if it doesn't, it's still more in the awe camp than the depressed/anxious camp, simply because you're feeling receptive. If you weren't feeling receptive at that spot, to that object, then you would feel more flatness/fear.

6) When that "spot" of openness shifts or dissolves (or just moves, like the man descending into the subway), then start over and find another spot.

The point of this exercise is to sensitize you and your brain to the experience—not the belief or faith or wish—of openness, whether more on the dread side, or the wonder side of awe. If depression and anxiety were hands, then they would be in constant states of clenching. Awe, if it were a hand, would be open, allowing the awe-some object to just rest on your hand.

Actively looking for awe is, like a pianist coming to identify notes by ear, actively sensitizing yourself to and practicing the state of openness.

Also, awe is a particular emotional response to something that is very real: we are thoroughly the vastness we see. To practice feeling awe, we are also retraining our depressive/anxious beliefs—again, through direct, visceral experience. Instead of, "I'm worthless, small, cut off," our minds, through the direct reality that awe responds to, becomes, "I'm part of the vastness, I have purpose, I am welcomed."

Really. You need to be somewhat ready, but after that, the mind and brain cannot forget the direct experience of reality, when it directly contradicts your beliefs. I can say the world is flat, loudly and passionately, but when I fly due west and eventually find myself back at my starting point, your mind wants to bend to the experienced truth.

I recently was tasked with pulling weeds in a garden, and was given a hoe after my initial pulling resulted in just a pile of the weed tops. Awe is like that hoe for depression and anxiety: it scoops under to the roots and pulls them up, one by one. The direct experience, over time—hence the emphasis on practice—will overpower the thought-based beliefs of insufficiency and fear.

If you suffer from anxiety and depression, then you know them very well. Now sit still and look for where they are not, and rest there.

**Here is another exercise in the cultivation of awe:**

1) Get comfortable and give yourself a little block of time so you can be reflective, without feeling rushed.

2) Think about something utterly mundane. E.g., the TV. The sky. A fingernail.

3) Contemplate the object and describe to yourself how it works. Keep working through the levels of explanation. For instance, with the TV: you plug it in and push the power button. Electricity flows from the wall socket to the TV. Electricity comes from the local generating plant through copper wires. The plant generates energy by burning coal. Coal was formed by certain geological processes millions of years ago. And so on....

4) Keep going until you start experiencing (not just thinking, but feeling) the sense of interconnection and bigness. That is, you begin experiencing some measure of awe.

Here's my example, coming from recent readings of neurobiology: I am contemplating the image of this computer I'm using. The steps I can think of are: light is projected from the screen, enters the eyes and registers on certain cells; an electro-chemical signal/vibration transfers to the brain's visual centers, and then I see an image. But as I think this through, I realize that there's no screen on which it projects; it simply arises somewhere and somehow in the mind. The mind depends on the organic brain. The brain has a several million year history.

For me, when I rest with that, I get a sense of vast mystery, and incredible complexity, and something approaching a sense of magic. That is, awe.

I saw the magicians Penn and Teller do a stage bit where they demonstrate the steps of a magic routine, first as trick, then as show-and-tell. Knowing how it was done—look, it's like this and this and then this happens, voila!— did not *at all* take the magic out of it. Because the magic is in the fact that it *can be done*;  the awe is in experiencing the fact that such complexity actually exists, and that it's both an *it* and a *me*.  You can know how the cigarette disappears, but letting yourself experience the routine in all its details and as something happening right now—that's where you find the awe in the most common of things.

Made in the USA
Charleston, SC
06 October 2011